Navigating Life:
Commonsense Reflections
for the Voyage

Joseph G. Langen, Ph.D.

Sliding Otter Publications
www.slidingotter.com
LeRoy, NY

Joseph G. Langen

Sliding Otter Publications

5 Franklin Ave.

Leroy, NY 14482

www.slidingotter.com

2009

Foreword

Men go abroad to wonder at the heights of mountains,
at the huge waves of the sea, at the long courses of the rivers,
at the vast compass of the ocean, at the circular motions of the stars;
and they pass by themselves without wondering.

~St. Augustine~

Life is an adventure. You can ignore it and let life's winds blow you where they will. You can complain about the trip. Or you can embrace your travels and make the best of them. I can't help you with the first two choices. If you choose the third option I have some provisions for your journey.

I will share with you suggestions for how you can better appreciate life. I also have some thoughts about how people choose to conduct their lives. Spirituality to me means "Awakening to the goodness and joy for which you were created." Following are reflections on how to live a spiritual life in this sense.

We have some extraordinary powers as humans. I offer you some thoughts on how to use them. We are social beings and, like it or not, live in society. I offer some thoughts about how to manage social life. We are creatures with feelings. Here are some ways to make good use of them. We all have talents and I have some ideas about putting them to good use. Life can be stressful but you can use it to move ahead rather than let it paralyze you.

I would like to introduce you to some interesting people I have met in my life voyage. I also have some reflections for you on communicating with others, handling relationships, understanding people different from us and people we would like to avoid. Finally I suggest a few values which affect our life outlook, values, emotions and relationships.

This book is dedicated to Haley Civiletti, Michael "Smokie" Callahan, Steve D'Annunzio, Rev. Richard Gill, Mary Anne Graney, Michael Napoleone, Lucille Rider, Pat Smith, Rose and Russ VanValkenburg and all the others whose lives have touched me and inspired these reflections.

Joseph G. Langen

Thanks to Carol Gomborone and Gerry Lanning for the tireless support of my efforts.

Table of Contents

Joseph G. Langen

Chapter 1

Appreciating Life Around Us

Our world is full of unexplored marvels. We pass by them every day. These reflections encourage you to slow down, notice life's treasures, and enjoy them rather than rushing through life. I encourage gratitude for life's magic, the angels in your life and your times of good fortune.

*****

The World of Blooming Buzzing Confusion

Try to find your deepest issue in every confusion
and abide by that.

D. H. Lawrence

I was sitting on my porch the other day watching trees blooming and cars buzzing by. I thought of how the nineteenth century psychologist William James described the world as babies first see it, a world of "blooming, buzzing confusion." Other psychologists have since speculated that babies can make more sense of the world than William James first thought. The dispute does not seem to have ever been settled to anyone's satisfaction. But then, babies aren't prone to lengthy explanations of their world view.

As adults, our world still seems to consist of blooming, buzzing and everything in between. Trees, flowers and plants slowly and gracefully unfold to share their beauty with us. People often buzz by, not wanting to share anything with us. They just wish we would get out of their way.

I have wondered lately where everyone is heading in such a rush. If we work ourselves into a lather trying to save a few minutes, what are these few minutes like when we finally get them? Can we enjoy them or do we need them to catch our breath after rushing to wherever we are headed?

Sometimes I think we are preoccupied with where we are coming from and where we are going, forgetting to enjoy the journey in between. I remember when I was young and our family would sometimes take a ride in the country. We weren't trying to get away from anything in particular or heading any place special. The ride itself was the whole point of the adventure.

What would it be like if we looked at our lives as a ride in the country? What if we got our minds off what we were trying to accomplish with our lives, even for a little while, and instead concentrated on enjoying the journey?

We don't often think to do this. Sometimes it is easier after a major illness or other setback. We are reminded that we won't be here forever. Even if we win the rat race, we are still rats.

We can slow down from time to time or even stop to enjoy our lives rather than letting them slip by as we race to our next destination. On holidays, we tend to take time out from our hectic pace, but often we find chores to occupy us rather than spending time with the treadmill turned off. We can even fret our way through vacations. We work hard to make sure we are having fun rather than just letting the vacation happen.

Do you remember the Simon and Garfunkel suggestion "Slow down, you're movin' too fast" from The 59th Street Bridge Song? I think they had the same reaction to the bridge that I had to the traffic whizzing by my porch. Our lives lie in the space between where we start and where we end. Don't let your life get away.

Life Lab Lessons:

- When was the last time you took time out from your busy schedule to just enjoy life?

- What was it like?

- When do you plan to do it again?

- What do you think you might have missed while rushing through your life?

- What would it be like to live your whole life in this moment rather than constantly pushing yourself toward the next goal?

Nourish and Preserve Your Sense of Wonderment

*The possession of knowledge does not kill
the sense of wonder and mystery.
There is always more mystery.*

~Anaïs Nin~

Recently I found myself at a funeral home following the sudden death of a friend, Mary Anne Graney. Near the guest book was a stack of cards and the invitation to write favorite memories of her to share with her family. I stopped to recall memories of her.

My first thought was her ability to make everyone she met feel special. This trait, in my mind, made her special. It was not quite what I wanted to write, but the right words to describe what set her aside from other people did not come to me.

This morning I woke up realizing what I wanted to say. What was unique about her was her ever present sense of wonderment. Hers was a rare gift which I have noticed in only one other person on a regular basis. I can't recall a conversation with her in which she did not display her gift.

I don't think I would have recognized her gift had I had not learned about it from a priest I knew long ago, Father Augustine

Paul. It is a little hard to define but it has also been described as "thinking with a child's mind," or openness to experience and suspending judgment.

Cynics would call this approach to life naïve. Life is serious. We are playing for keeps. This is no time to fool around. Some people become caught up in the practical. They leave no time for things which are interesting, fascinating or even wonderful. Dreamers can be annoying to people who want to avoid the nonsense and just get things done.

Religions have often started out with a sense of awe at creation and ended up becoming a justification for the way of life of its adherents. The writings of early explorers describe the wonders of their discoveries. Often the lands they discovered have become the focus of squabbles about how to use the natural resources they contain. A beautiful maple tree, which I admired for years each morning over coffee, was finally gobbled up by machines to make way for a store parking lot.

I have written before of the sense of wonderment children have. I still remember a photo I took of my son around age two, running through a field holding up a daisy he had found.

We become jaded by our pursuit of careers, possessions and money, known as the rat race. This is a good descriptive term which suggests roaring ahead full steam toward a goal with no awareness of our surroundings. Sometimes we lose sight of the goal and are aware only of the rat race.

We have another choice. We can reassess our goals and decide whether they are worth all of our energy. We can work toward a balance in our lives, taking some time to appreciate the wonders around us. We can also share our sense of wonderment with our more frantic fellow life travelers. Mary Anne, thanks for your example.

Life Lab Lessons

- What makes some people special to you?
- How is your life better for your association with them?
- What have you learned from their lives?
- How could your life be more like theirs?

- Incorporate their best traits into your daily life.

The Magic of Everyday Life

Surprise is the greatest gift which life can grant us.

~Boris Pasternak~

I learn daily of the number of American soldiers dying in Iraq. I hear less about the much larger number of dead Iraqis. I read of the ingrained hatreds among groups around the world and wonder how things could have come to this. The problems seem overwhelming. How could the world be a different place?

Just when things seem most hopeless, something happens to remind me that life is still full of wonderful surprises. They do not appear every minute or maybe they do and I just don't notice them. When I sense them, they remind me that people are on earth to enjoy what God has put before them rather than to find more efficient ways to destroy each other.

I have seen the most glorious sunset I could imagine at Sunset Beach in Oahu. I was present at the births of three healthy babies entrusted to my safekeeping. I looked down on the Grand Canyon from thirty five thousand feet in the air.

I have heard Dvorak's Symphony From the New World played in a park in Pittsburgh and the Queen of the Night aria from The Magic Flute sung in concert as well as whistled on the street. I have heard my grandson Joey talking a mile a minute after having to learn sign language because of his delayed speech.

I have smelled the scent of holly flowers meant to attract bumblebees. I have enjoyed the aroma of honeysuckle pervading the countryside and the fragrance of night blooming cereus wafting `across my front porch.

I have tasted Evil Jungle Prince sitting in Keo's Honolulu Restaurant among the orchids, sipped Sangria at a modest restaurant in Gijon, Spain and relished Pat Davis cakes at family celebrations.

I swam in the Sea of Cortez, felt my hair stand on end as I touched a Van de Graf generator and had my hand tickled by a salamander scooting across my palm.

These are a few of the sensory experiences which have surprised me over the years. I did not plan or expect any of them to happen and they are by no means the only pleasant surprises I have encountered during my journey through life.

Thomas Moore in *The Re-Enchantment of Everyday Life* helps us regain a sense of wonderment about the many mysteries of the world waiting for our exploration and appreciation. Diane Ackerman in *A Natural History of the Senses* gives us a context for appreciating all that our senses bring to our life experience.

I am sure there are many delights I have encountered in passing but have not dwelt upon sufficiently and many others which I have not taken the time to even notice. I hope I can set aside my concerns to better notice the delights God has placed along my path. I also hope that delight in nature can help turn the world people's attention from its conflicts and give them a context in which to start appreciating each other better.

Life Lab Lessons

- Recall what has delighted you over the years.
- Think of the last delight you encountered.
- Which of your life experiences means the most to you?
- Think about how you could delight someone you care about.
- Set aside some time for wonderment about the world you live in.

Things That Make Me Feel Grateful

*Let the man, who would be grateful
think of repaying a kindness
even while receiving it.*

~Seneca~

Several years ago I started following the example of Henry Thoreau. He made it a practice not to get out of bed until he had written down things for which he was grateful that day. I usually have a cup of coffee but like to make my list before doing anything else. In honor of Thanksgiving, I thought I would use this article to share some of the things for which I am grateful

Thank you God for:

- The cloth-bound journal I found at the Bunch of Grapes Bookstore.

- The wonderful sunrises and sunsets this year which never fail to gladden my heart and raise my spirits. Even on gloomy days, I know that sooner or later one or the other will eventually grace the sky.

- The warm summer sand at Gay Head Beach on Martha's Vineyard and the lazy waves lapping at the shore.

- Attending two delightful weddings in one summer and meeting new people.

- The many teens honored at the Bishop McNulty Awards for parish service and the adults honored for working with youth.

- Sharing my perceptions of the world with my brother Bob and his understanding of what is important to me.

- My mother's acceptance and caring for every person I have ever brought to her door.

- My friend Smokey, the joy he brought to my life and his many friends I had the chance to meet if only briefly.

- Being able to publish three books and write a newspaper column for five years without losing my perseverance.

- Inspiration for my writing each time I get my fingers moving.

- My muse, Calliope, and my ongoing conversations with her.

- Attending the celebration of Rose's and Russ's sixtieth wedding anniversary.

- Seeing Aunt Lucille's zest for life well into her eighties.

- Mike and Joe's delight in each other's company.

- Matt's ability to commune with nature whether anyone is around or not.

- Visiting England, Spain and Portugal.

- Peter's prolific pursuit of his artistic ability.

- Sue's professional competence and community contributions.

- Becky's continuous caring for everyone she meets following her grandmother's example.

- Coming to a decision about Medicare coverage and its many options.

- Delightful conversations with many people I never thought I would meet.

- Sailing on cruises among the Caribbean islands in February.

- Having owned my own sailboat.

- Visiting a sugar plantation in Barbados.

- Rediscovering my friend Gerry and knowing I can count on his constant support and encouragement.

- A sense of prosperity after years of worrying about money.

- A growing sense of my spirituality and coming to terms with it.

- Visiting St. John the Divine in New York.

- My joints working well again after several years of feeling almost crippled.
- Carol's love, support and acceptance of me no matter what.

Life Lab Lessons:

- Think of some of the things for which you are grateful.
- List the people who have meant the most to you.
- Tell the ones who are still living how you feel about them.
- Do something in honor of the ones who have died.
- Consider writing down a few things each day for which you are grateful.

The Care and Feeding of Angels

Do not forget to entertain strangers, for by so doing some have unwittingly entertained angels.

~Hebrews 13:2~

I wrote in the past about the angels among us, working quietly to make our lives better and easing the strain of our life challenges. They are often unacknowledged and sometimes unnoticed.

Even though I refer to them as angels, they are not just spirits. They have human needs too. However, in their efforts to care for the rest of us, they often forget about their own needs. They are just as prone to stress and burn-out as we are, although they are probably less attuned to these signs, since they are so focused on what others need.

I have often heard from people who are good listeners that no one cares about their concerns. No one imagines anything could ever bother them. Caretakers sometimes seem indestructible, or maybe it is just our wishful thinking.

Whose responsibility is it to care for the angels in our lives? First, it is their responsibility. Everyone knows that a car will

9

break down quickly without regular service and maintenance. While people are not machines, they also need nourishment, rest, exercise, appreciation and support.

If you are an angel, stop to think how much you are doing for everyone else and also what you need. What do you do for yourself? In your efforts to care for everyone else, do you forget to take care of yourself? Do you listen to what your body is telling you? Do you pay attention to your feelings of stress, exhaustion and loneliness, or do you try to carry on as if you don't have any of these feelings?

You deserve to take care of your body, and especially of your spirit. Take time to sit quietly and be aware of your requirements as you do for everyone else. You have needs too. Once you are aware of them, set aside some time for yourself. It may seem selfish, but unless you do, you won't remain helpful to others.

If you are not an angel but have one or more of them in your life, stop to think about what they may need. Encourage them to consider their own desires and what may please them. There may also be things you can do for them. It might be hard to figure out what they want since they do not often make their wishes known. They may seem like they can go on forever taking care of you as they always have.

It helps to let them know you appreciate all they do for you instead of taking them for granted. But this might not be enough, since appreciation might tempt them to work all the harder.

You might watch them and see what they need. They might appreciate being reminded to take time for themselves. You could let them know they don't have to be of service immediately or on call twenty four hours a day. Or you could find a way to be their angel at least on occasion.

Life Lab Lessons

- Discover who your angels are.
- Think about how they have enriched your life.
- Make sure you thank them.
- What could your angels use from you in return?

- Do it for them.

Thank Your Friends for Their Help

*Do not save your loving speeches for your friends till they are
dead.
Do not write them on their tombstones;
speak them rather now instead.*

~Anna Cummins~

Dear Pat,

A while ago when I was visiting your house, you made a comment to me which seemed like no big deal. You had seen an ad in the paper for volunteers to take part in a study of rheumatoid arthritis. I have been struggling with arthritis for a couple years and thought I might have the rheumatoid variety, but so far had been unsuccessful in finding a rheumatologist.

I had been taking Celebrex and Tylenol for a while with little relief. But lately, every time I moved my shoulder I felt a crunch like I had no cartilage. I was about to resume my search for a rheumatologist, which last time led to a dead end.

The morning after you told me about the study, I called the number you gave me and set up an appointment. I was screened and accepted for the study and finally began treatment. The morning after I started, I woke up with not an ache, pain or discomfort anywhere in my body. I considered it a miracle and felt like a new person.

After being in the study for a couple weeks, I looked around my house and discovered stacks of unfinished projects. When I thought about it, I realized I had been depressed for some time. I work with many depressed people and somehow did not recognize the symptoms in myself.

Every morning since, I have woken up thanking God for leading scientists to the discovery of the medications I now take, for leading me to your house that afternoon, and for your thoughtfulness in telling me about the study. I think I sometimes take others' help for granted. Maybe it takes something this intrusive to make me realize friends make many gestures which improve my life in less dramatic ways.

We all get busy thinking about our own needs and how things affect us. I have had concerns that our society has been becoming more selfish and people are becoming so preoccupied with their own needs that they do not pay attention to those around them. It is sometimes hard to remember that people traveling their life paths next to us are also preoccupied with their own concerns at the people next to us and gain some appreciation of their struggles. Going further, we can find and share something which might help them a little. Getting in touch with their needs also opens up a channel between us and them and makes a connection with all the people they are connected to. The information you shared with me about the study led to my finding out about the study medications. I shared what I discovered with a colleague, who in turn passed it on to someone she knew with rheumatoid arthritis whom I have never met.

When I think back over my life, I can recall times when I was helpful to others, sometimes in ways which made a dramatic difference in their lives and sometimes in ways which may have made their way just a little easier. I have learned two lessons from your kindness. One is to acknowledge my appreciation for others efforts on my behalf. The other is to extend myself when I can be helpful to others and make their lives a little better.

Life Lab Lessons

- What have been the most difficult times in your life?
- Which of your friends have been most there for you at those times?
- How did they help?
- Did you thank them properly?
- It's not too late.

Following the Relay for Life

We cannot direct the wind but we can adjust the sails.

~Author Unknown~

Recently I found myself in the Spencerport High School sports stadium. Tents rose throughout the infield; a band warmed up. The high school color guard marched in to the beat of their drummers. Among them I found the names of Carol, her younger sister and her nephew. Around me was a sea of people wearing purple shirts, all displaying a message on the back, "Survivor."

Everyone had gathered for the American Cancer Society Relay for Life, in honor of those who had survived cancer, those who had not and those who might eventually face it. We had been invited to attend several times in the past, but had not ever done so for one reason or another. This year was different.

The announcer read the names of all the survivors present, their type of cancer and how long they had survived. Among them were a five year old boy, people in wheel chairs and women with the tell-tale scarves covering their chemotherapy-induced hair loss. As their names were read, they assembled on the track. After the reading, they walked together around the track as those who loved them looked on in silence.

Toward the front walked Carol, her older sister Sharon and brother-in-law Gary. I took this in stride until they walked by me. I had not known Carol's mother or sister Marie who had died of cancer before we started dating. I knew Carol's nephew, Tommy, who fought cancer for three years to have more time with his children Haley and Andrew.

For the past six months, Carol took on her own fight with cancer while I did what I could, often feeling helpless. We both focused on what had to be done and had little time to think about how we felt about the ordeal.

After supporting her through her diagnosis, surgery, radiation and chemotherapy, I stood beside the track watching Carol walk with the sea of other survivors. For the first time since her diagnosis, my emotions overcame me and tears came to my eyes. I felt remnants of my initial fear and sorrow that her family pattern of cancer had finally caught up with her as well as respect for her courage in facing her ordeal and gratitude that she had survived it.

I often wondered about cancer but had never taken it seriously in the past. My first question to her radiologist was, "Why do people get cancer?" I have seen and heard explanations on many levels but have yet to find one which adequately answers my question. Cancer has been around for centuries, but not to the extent it is today. Our environment, lifestyles and diet all seem to play parts. Still it is not clear, at least to me, why some people get cancer and others don't.

Carol's encounter has brought me to a new respect for life, how precious it is and my need to cherish it. I don't think I will ever look at Carol again and take her for granted.

Life Lab Lessons

- Think about how you live your life and how you treat your body?

- What would your body say about how you treat it?

- Find out what you can do to protect yourself from cancer.

- If you have lost someone to cancer, live part of your life in his or her honor.

- If you love any cancer survivors, find ways to show them how much they mean to you.

Chapter 2

How You Conduct Your Life

We have only one chance to live our lives. We can change
course if we don't like where we are headed. Here are some
reflections to help you appreciate nature, what your life is about,
choices facing you and some alternative ways to live your life. I
hope you enjoy your journey.

*****

On the Nature and Meaning of Things

Life is like riding a bicycle.
To keep your balance you must keep moving.

~Albert Einstein~

My new space is smaller than my old one. Some things had to
go. For the most part, decisions were fairly easy. Having retired
as a psychologist, many of my psychological trappings became
expendable. Books, tests and files headed for the library sale or
to the trash. Would I need any of these in the future? Possible,
but not likely.

I left most of my monastic effects behind long ago and gradually
divested myself of the rest one by one over the years. All that
remains is my Latin dictionary and Psalter from which I once
chanted. When I wrote a memoir about my seminary life, I
wished I had kept my writings for reference but I managed

without them, relying instead on the kind assistance and steel trap memory of my good friend Gerry.

I have kept a few books from my psychology days: a diagnostic manual, two books on personality types and a few volumes on practical wisdom. I had a twinge of regret parting with some of the others. Then it occurred to me that anything I need in the future will most likely be available on the Internet or through inter-library loan.

What else did I keep? My computer and some of my furniture made the trip. So did my published columns and books, writing and publishing references and art materials. My plants also came in out of the cold for the winter.

As I sit on the couch, I can see everything of importance to me, together in one space for the first time in my life. I find this comforting. So what do my things mean to me? The ones I brought give me a sense of continuity with my past and memories to guide me into the future.

My move gave me the opportunity to consider the meaning of the things which follow us through life until we decide to let them go. I once read a saying, "The one who dies with the most toys wins." I realized this was quite childish. We can die clinging to things we valued during our lives. No matter how tightly we cling to them, they don't accompany us to the next phase of our existence beyond the grave. They all pass to our loved ones or end up in a garage sale or the trash.

Our things are the least of our legacy. More important is how we have lived and the impression our lives have left on those touched by knowing us. I try to keep this in mind on a daily basis.

Life Lab Lessons

- Look around to see what things surround you.
- Consider the memories attached to each of them.
- Which of your things connect you to people you care about the most?
- Tell special people what they mean to you.
- Think about what you would like as your legacy.

Coming to Terms with Life's Mysteries

*There is something precious in our being mysteries to ourselves,
in our being able ever to see through even the person who is
closest to our heart and to reckon with him as though he were a
logical proposition or a problem in accounting.*

~Rudolf Bultman~

When I was a child I thought I knew everything. As a young man, I came to realize I didn't know everything but thought I could understand and make sense of anything. Over the years, I have come to realize there are some things I will never understand. I think of them as life's mysteries.

One of them has to do with the universe. How do all the heavenly spheres stay in balance year after year? Maybe astronomers or physicists understand the balance, but to me it remains precarious and mysterious.

The universe inside the atom is equally mysterious to me. Left to themselves, subatomic particles stay balanced and keep spinning. Particle accelerators can create spectacular if short lived fireworks. Then there is atomic fission fueling power plants as well as nuclear warheads poised to threaten the survival of the world if someone gets crazy enough. How can the world inside the atom be so fascinating as well as so fearsome?

In between the universe and the atom are a whole range of mysteries. The Bee Movie recently reminded me that theoretically bees can't fly, yet they do. Migrating birds somehow find their way from a pond on one continent to a lake on another. A recent theory suggests birds can detect and even see the earth's magnetic fields. Even if true, that doesn't entirely resolve the mystery of migration for me. And what of whales and butterflies which also migrate?

It is not just nature that's mysterious. I have sailed upwind in a sailboat and sometimes still wonder how I did it. Despite my sailing experience, windsurfing remains a mystery at least for anything longer than five seconds.

Computers are also mysterious. How does moving a mouse with your hand change where the pointer is on the screen? When I first studied computers, I learned that all they can do is say yes or no, on or off, one or zero. Yet these simple operations have connected the continents through the World Wide Web.

I also wonder how maple trees, bees and worms can give us tons of maple syrup, honey, and silk with no threat to their survival. When I was in grammar school I learned that it would probably not be too long before the world ran out of oil. Yet the supply seems almost inexhaustible.

What about the glorious colors in the changing leaves each Fall? And what of the breathtaking sunrises and sunsets around the world each day? None of these seem to serve any useful purpose other than to make us delight in them.

I could go on, but I think you get the point. We are surrounded by fascinating and wonderful events, many of which we tend to take for granted. Maybe it's time to stop and marvel at the parts of our universe which entrance us.

Life Lab Lessons

- Think of what creates a sense of wonder in you on your daily rounds.
- Take time to stop and delight in your wonderment.
- Balance your time of worry with time to let the world fascinate you.
- Think of what enthralls you about other people.
- Let people know when they delight you.

Life Choices: Love, Fear or Power

People will forget what you said,
and people will forget what you did,
but they will never forget how you made them feel.

~Astraea~

Did you know you had choices of how to live? Choosing love means being aware of the needs of others around you, knowing what you have to offer them and doing what you can to help them meet their goals. Choosing fear means not getting close enough to know what others need and avoiding them as much as possible. Choosing power means focusing on your own needs and making sure they get met by taking control of others.

All three styles depend on how you feel about yourself. If you like who you are and are confident in yourself, you may choose love as your predominant driving force. The less sure of yourself you are, the more you may be inclined toward fear or power.

Despite the recent election talk of values and morality, not far below the surface in most of us is a desire to have others think and act the way we do. We don't want to hear what others believe unless it matches what we believe. I know this is true, at least for me. I avoid political conversations with people, even friends, who I knew do not see things my way.

Even after elections are over and there is talk on both sides of reconciliation, we are still quite polarized in our understanding of where our country should be headed. Those who won see the election as a mandate to pursue their vision. Those who lost plan to regroup, focusing their efforts on the next election. While there is strength in diversity of opinion, there can also be divisiveness and polarization. The challenge of democracy is to pursue our own goals while respecting the right of others to pursue theirs.

Sometimes our differences are only apparent. The words we use can cloud the issues. Opposing positions might not be as far apart as we think, but are couched in terms which make them appear incompatible. Listening to each other might help us realize we want the same things and can work together toward our mutual goals.

Sometimes there are radical differences in our positions so that it is not possible to have it both ways. We could fight it out, the winners having their way and the losers sulking in defeat. We could also examine our own position to see if it makes sense and whether we could make any changes which would, at least partially, satisfy the opposition.

Then we could take the time to listen to the other side, understanding what they want. While doing so we can be on the lookout for ways in which their position complements ours. With mutual understanding, compromise is more possible. Winning or losing without compromise can result in bitter feelings on both sides.

I am not in a position to preach about how we should live our lives as good citizens. I have not been a prime example of what to do and have tended to isolate myself, talking only with those who agree with me. Having considered all this, I plan to think about how sensible my goals are and to see where I can be more flexible. I plan to listen to opposing positions and look for ways they can complement mine. I plan to seek dialog rather than isolation or confrontation.

Life Lab Lessons

- Could you seek mutually satisfying decisions rather than reacting automatically?
- How often are you tempted to react in a negative way?
- How can you remind yourself of your choices?
- Do you need to make some changes?
- Try it today.

The Simple and the Complex in Our Lives

Simplicity is making the journey of this life
with just baggage enough.

~Charles Dudley Warner~

Have you ever stopped to watch young children going about their business? At first, life is very simple. They feel good when they are full, warm, dry and safe. They feel bad when they are hungry, cold, wet or threatened. They don't stop to think about how they feel, they just react immediately.

As we age, life becomes more complicated. By the time we get to school, we start thinking about whether others like us, whether we are smart enough or whether we have the things our playmates have. Later we face decisions about what to do with our lives, the prospect of a life partner and how to spend our time. We would all like to be happy, but how do we get there?

We are constantly bombarded by TV, phone or e-mail ads suggesting things we can't live without. Loneliness sometimes prompts us to surround ourselves with people we would be better off without. People might expect things of us that would take more time to do than we have available. If we are surrounded by enough things and busy enough, we are tempted to think we will be happy. But there can still be a sense that something is missing if we slow down enough to notice.

If we put aside the things, people and activities for a while, we will notice that there is a part of ourselves all our own. Many people don't take the time to stop and ask themselves who they really are and what they are doing on earth. Life is not a popularity contest, a garage sale or a race to see who can get the most done.

If we peel off the other people, things and activities like layers of an onion skin, what is left of us? We finally get to who we are and are meant to be. It is hard to find time to look at ourselves this way. We have too much to do. People who are sick in bed and can't do much of anything sometimes use the time to reassess their lives. Some people take vacations, days off or spend in a retreat to get some perspective. Have you ever spent time alone to get to know yourself? It can help you realize what is important to you. You can also discover what distracts you from living your life.

We don't have to make this an occasional exercise followed by a return to our hectic lives. We can work to make simplicity our focus and eliminate things, people and activities which make our lives more complicated and distract us from living the way we see best.

Life Lab Lessons

- Set aside some time to think about your life.

- List what is really important to you.

- Think about the people in your lives who help you reach your goals.

- Decide which of your possessions and activities help you along your path.

- Make some tough choices.

If You Really Knew Me

Man is never alone. Acknowledged or unacknowledged,
that which dreams through him is always there to support him
from within.

~Laurence van der Post~

Once I watched a segment on Oprah called High School Challenge. A group of high school students spent the day getting to know themselves and others by finishing the sentence, "If you really knew me..." Predictably, they started with superficial statements revealing only the obvious. As the day progressed, they began to reveal more personal concerns and eventually got to the secrets which deeply troubled them.

I think most of us are not very different from high school students. It is not easy for us to reveal our secret fears and insecurities. We might look for ways to hide from being noticed, remaining wallflowers at the dance of life. We might be aggressive as a way to conceal our insecurities, in the manner of bullies. We might choose the path of those who tease others, focusing on their shortcomings so that ours are not so apparent.

How would we finish the statement, "If you really knew me...?" How honest would we be? We would probably start with safe statements, revealing little about ourselves. As we feel safer, we might start sharing more personal information and eventually get to the concerns with deeply trouble us.

We might admit that we never felt loved, at least not as much as others in our family. We might admit our embarrassment at what makes us different from others: our skin color, our physical appearance, or our physical, mental and emotional shortcomings. We might admit feeling that we have not accomplished as much as we would like and probably never will. We might express feeling disappointed by not becoming what others expect of us.

Voicing these concerns might be a revelation to us as well as to others. We often hide these issues from ourselves so we don't have to face them. We try to ignore them or pretend they don't exist. Even if we can't see them clearly, we still trip over them when we least expect it. We all have fears and insecurities buried deep within us. We can develop a shell for protection as some animals do, or develop weapons such as claws, quills or poisons to keep others at bay. None of these approaches will make us feel any better about ourselves. They are just tools we use to keep from being hurt. In the long run they keep us isolated from others.

What if we could find a way to be open with others about our insecurities and make it safe for them to share theirs with us? Maybe it would be a way for us to contribute to a less hostile world. Maybe it would be easier for us to live in peace with each other.

Life Lab Lessons

- Make a list of what troubles you.

- Make further lists until you have some deep feelings about what you write.

- Take the risk of sharing your list with someone you trust.

- Make it safe for someone to share his or her concerns with you.

- Talk about what you have in common and how you can help each other.

Respecting our Wisdom and Judgment

*Wisdom is meaningless until your own experience has given it
meaning and there is wisdom in the selection of wisdom.*

~Bergen Evans~

Have you ever thought about how we end up doing the things we
do? Have you ever acted a certain way and then thought to
yourself, "That was dumb?" I would guess all of us have from
time to time. Those of us with experience as parents have often
watched our children getting into trouble by not thinking first. I
would dare say one of the main jobs of parents is to get their
children to think before they act.

Knowledge is a collection of facts. Wisdom is the way we
evaluate our actions and put them into perspective. Judgment
involves thinking before acting. People sometimes are able to
recite all the facts about what will happen if they act a certain
way but don't take the consequences seriously. Criminals are
well aware of the consequences of their crimes but somehow
don't think the rules apply to them.

Sometimes we make up our own rules as we go along. We
expect one thing from everyone else but have our own private set
of rules for our actions. I think we sometimes forget why there
are rules in the first place or don't consider them as applying to
us.

When we were children, the ultimate authority lay in our parents.
Even if we did not understand the rules or want to accept them,
our parents said these were the rules "because I said so." As we
became older, most of us took the time to understand why we
have rules. It is a way of knowing what to expect from others
and what others expect from us.

Respecting the rules is a way of respecting each other. Could you
imagine driving down the road and not knowing whether another
driver will stop at a red light, drive on the expected side of the
road or obey traffic signs?

Wisdom is not always written down as laws or rules. Much of
wisdom is the result of learning over generations about
consequences and the best way to do things. Some of this

wisdom ends up in the laws of our civilization but some of it is handed down in our family traditions. We can learn everything the hard way, but we save ourselves a great deal of trouble by learning from our forebears. The problem is that it takes a certain amount of wisdom to recognize the wisdom of others. We sometimes think we know best and can learn everything we need to on our own.

We might be able to find our own path, but it is like clearing a way through a jungle when there is a nearby path waiting for us to follow it. Do we really want to spend all that time learning what others have learned and rediscovering paths which our ancestors have forged? We do have a choice.

Life Lab Lessons

- Think about what lessons you have learned from your parents and grandparents.

- Compare what happens when you listen to wisdom or act impulsively.

- Who are the wise people in your life now?

- What can you learn from them?

- What would it take to share your wisdom with others?

Getting Ahead of Ourselves

Having spent the better part of my life
trying either to relive the past
or experience the future before it arrives,
I have come to believe that
in between these two extremes is peace.

~Author Unknown~

A recent letter to the editor complained about a prominent Halloween store display in August. Department store catalogs and circulars, TV ads and other advertising also focus on what is coming rather than what is happening now.

Maybe this is all part of the rush to get to the next stage of our lives. Cars sprinting past my house every morning remind me of our rush to live in the future rather than in the present.

Are our lives so empty that we need to look past the current moment? Do we expect the future to be an improvement on the present? We forget that the past is over and the future is just a possibility. We don't even know if we will be alive when the future arrives.

We can't change the past and we can't control or even predict the future. We can manage only the time we have right now and we do have a choice of what we do at this moment. We create our past by how we handle the present moment. We can influence our future by forging a path for our next steps.

So what can we do about right now? First, we can stop looking backward or forward at least for a little while. We can think about where we are right now. Most of us have heard the expression "living in the moment." Is this just a saying or is there something to it?

We are wasting our time thinking about what might have been or what could be. That is unless we use our past to guide our current decisions or use our future goals to enlighten our current choices.

When we examiner our past, it is easy to take ourselves to task for not doing things better. "How could I be so dumb?" We sometimes spend quite a bit of time fretting about the future as well. I have met more than a few people whose mantra is, "What if..." People paralyzed by what might happen find it hard to make any decisions at all.

Sometimes the present moment doesn't call for a decision on our part. We can take a deep breath and enjoy its peace. How many such moments can you remember in your lifetime, or in the past week?

Most of us carry concerns around with us such as health, money or difficult people waiting in our path. But do we have to spend every moment of our lives wringing our hands? If we take time to enjoy a particular moment, our world will not fall apart. Instead we might find that our moments of reflection refresh us and sometimes give us a new perspective.

Life Lab Lessons

- When was the last time you took a moment just to exist?
- What was it like?
- Did the sky fall down?
- Try scheduling a few moments of peace for yourself.
- If you enjoy it, make it a habit.

Mommy, Are We There Yet?

Patience and perseverance have a magical effect
before which difficulties disappear and obstacles vanish.

~John Quincy Adams~

Do you remember hearing this plaintive question from the back seat or recall voicing it yourself? The words are quite familiar and express the boredom of a child waiting to get somewhere so the fun can begin. How often do you feel bored? How did you get that way?

Boredom is defined as "the state of being weary and restless through lack of interest." If you think about it, you weren't born bored. Did you ever notice how curious babies are about every sight, sound and movement in their vicinity? Nothing escapes their attention. As children get older and start to walk, their curiosity increases. If children are encouraged to continue exploring the wonders of their world, they remain curious and fascinated. If they are discouraged from exploring, they might end up feeling bored.

As adults, we may become "weary and restless." Our lack of interest in our surroundings may come from discouragement of our explorations. We may be told to concentrate on our work rather than wasting our time with foolishness. Poetry, fiction or music may be seen as distracting us from our real studies or from work.

We may place a high priority on financial success, accomplishment or acceptance by others. We may be so busy keeping our shoulder to the wheel, our ear to the ground and our nose to the grindstone that we miss the wonders of the world around us or inside us.

We may become so preoccupied with the world's troubles that we spend most of our time fretting about what the world has come to. There is no time left to enjoy ourselves. If we are bored, we have missed something and are not open to the opportunities along our way.

What can we do about it? The first step is to realize that we have become lost. Maybe we have forgotten, or never learned, why we are on earth at all. I have asked many people why they are here. Some people are quite clear on their mission in life, while others have no idea. In my experience, it is only the second group which tends to become bored.

If you have a purpose in life, it is hard to get bored. However if your purpose is material, it is easy to become exhausted. Consider two examples. One person has a goal of earning as much money as possible. This is an endless goal which never leads to a feeling of satisfaction. Another person has a goal of using God's gifts to make their own and other people's lives a little better each day. Following this goal and being successful with it allows the second person to sleep easily each night and wake up refreshed.

What are your goals? What do you want to accomplish in your lifetime? What do you want to accomplish today? Having worthwhile goals and pursuing them the best you can each day is invigorating and helps you start again tomorrow. If you can't identify any worthwhile goals for your life, think of some which can give you a focus. It's hard to be bored when you have found your own gifts and share them with others.

Life Lab Lessons

- When was the last time you approached your day with a sense of adventure?

- What did this curiosity feel like?

- Do you sometimes miss moments because you're busy looking forward to the next one?

- Do you live in the past, future or present?

- What can you do with the moment you are living in right now?

Commonsense Wisdom and the Cowboy Mentality

Generosity is another quality which, like patience, letting go, nonjudging and trust, provides a solid foundation for mindfulness practice. You might experiment with using the cultivation of generosity as a vehicle for deep self-observation and inquiry as well as an exercise in giving. A good place to start is with you. See if you can give yourself gifts that may be true blessings, such as self-acceptance, or some time each day with no purpose. Practice feeling deserving enough to accept these gifts without obligation-to simply receive from yourself, and from the universe.

~Jon Kabat Zinn~

For as long as I have been writing I have looked for ways to help people see the effect they have on others. I have also tried to help people see that the best way to meet their needs and reach their goals is by working to help others get what they want. If each of us lived in a cave and was capable of meeting all of our own needs, it would not matter so much how we treat others.

But we don't live in caves and our needs and wishes are interdependent with the needs and goals of others. We have what others want and others have what we want. If we had to provide all our own food, our diet would be quite meager. But what about our emotional needs? Some of us might be capable of going for a while without any human interaction. But even monks bow to each other on their silent walks. Knowing we are not alone makes our joy more intense and our sorrows more bearable.

So what does all this have to do with the cowboy mentality? News articles and reports tend to focus on how badly we treat each other. Senseless murders take page one. Sexual abuse of children became notorious among a few priests. Now teachers and other caretakers are picking up the slack. In our rush for security, we are pushing human rights to the side. We are moving toward being a nation of gunslingers, literally and figuratively.

When I studied world history, one lesson was that all great civilizations eventually crumble under their own weight. I did not want to believe this of my country and way of life. Now I am concerned about it and worry about the direction we seem to be taking as a society. Our needs are all that is important. What you want is only important to the extent that it gets me what I want.

I am not suggesting that our civilization has reached this point already. But the trend in that direction is disappointing and alarming to me. What will be left of us as a civilization if we continue to push each other out of our way and try to grab what we want without regard for each other?

What is the alternative? We can't leave taking the first step to others. Each of us must take the initiative in our own lives and do what we can to help each other. None of us can single-handedly erase disease, mental illness, poverty or crime. But we can make life a little better in small ways for those we encounter along our life's path. Are you willing to put your own needs aside, if ever so briefly, and consider for a moment what someone else might need?

Life Lab Lessons

- Think about what you really need in life.

- Stop to think what someone else might need.

- Can you help provide it in even some small way?

- Try doing something for someone without them knowing you did it.

- After trying this a few times, stop to see whether your view of yourself has changed.

What to Do When You Have No Luck At All

I find that the harder I work, the more luck I seem to have.

~John Heywood~

As I was planning this reflection, I thought of the line from the TV show, Hee Haw, "If it weren't for bad luck, I'd have no luck at all."

Sometimes our ordinary lives are interrupted by dramatic manifestations of good or bad fortune. We are prompted to step back from our routine and reexamine the course of our lives. We can go on for some time with no dramatic peaks or valleys. Usually when this happens, we fall into a routine, doing the same things, thinking the same thoughts and having the same feelings day after day. There is nothing to make us stop to reflect on our lives. We tend to blindly follow the course our life takes.

When things are going well there is little incentive to stop and reevaluate our lives. At other times when things are not going so well, we get stuck in a rut, accepting things as they are even though we would like them to be different.

We can continue to accept things as they are, and let our patterns remain unexamined indefinitely. I remember the story of a couple who ate liver every Thursday night for the first twenty five years of their marriage. When they stopped to consider their life together on their anniversary, the husband told his wife they had a great marriage except for her insistence on serving liver every Thursday. She told him she only served it because he seemed to like it. He responded that he only told her he liked it so he would not hurt her feelings. These two people continued an annoying but unnecessary habit which remained in place without being addressed for many years.

Even if things seem to be going well, it might be a good idea to take time once in a while to consider where we are headed, whether we are still satisfied with the course we have set, and whether our current behavior is taking us in a positive direction. To some extent, this is the motivation behind New Year's resolutions. We don't have to wait for a new year but could take some time out quarterly, monthly or even daily to briefly consider the course of our lives.

Stop to consider any changes you have made in your routine since the last time you thought about it. Ask yourself whether doing things differently is better than doing them the old way. Is there something you have always wanted to try but never felt you had the time, money or courage to pursue it? If you don't do it now, when will you?

Life Lab Lessons

- Do you like the direction your life is taking?
- Do you feel stuck in a rut?
- What would you like different in your life?
- What could you do to make your life better?
- When will you be ready to start?

Starting Over Once Again

Though no one can go back and make a brand new start, anyone can start from now and make a brand new ending.

~Carl Bard~

Now that I have packed what still matters to me and passed on to others what doesn't, where is my life headed from here? Lately I have thought of all the new beginnings in my life. I don't remember being born. My first memory was from age three, seeing the Capitol while changing trains in the middle of the night in Washington as my mother and I traveled to Miami where my father was stationed during World War Two.

We lived in a few other places, but mostly I remember my grandparents'' house in Dunkirk as my first home. When I was about six, our little family lived briefly with my Aunt Dottie and Uncle Fred in Newark, New York. Then we moved to our home in Rochester, a double house shared by my Aunt Marge and Uncle Ed and their family.

In 1951 we moved to Greece and our first new house. For the first time I faced leaving good friends and a house I thought would always be my home. I enjoyed being what help I could be to my father and several neighbors as they finished the upstairs, garage and driveway. I made new friends and settled down until the end of eighth grade again with no thoughts of ever moving.

Then I returned to Dunkirk for seminary and monastic life and another new adventure which lasted nine years in answer to what I thought was a call to the priesthood. Whether the call was a wrong number or whether I somehow fell short, I ended up back in Rochester with little sense of how to act as a young adult.

Somehow I managed college and university, finding a wife and starting a family as well as a number of professional jobs. Again, contrary to my expectations, I found myself divorced twelve years ago and moving to my now quickly emptying apartment. Memories of my transitional life remain, but many of the trappings are history.

Now what? I have learned enough about life to know I can't predict what will happen next. I have a few ideas. I plan to continue writing, painting, photography and travel. What else awaits me? If I knew, some of the adventure of my life would disappear. Fortunately, I have grown used to change, heading down paths which open up for me in unexpected directions and embarking on explorations I never anticipated.

I never expected to end up living with Carol when I met her years ago as a colleague. Yet here we are in the final phase of cementing our relationship by sharing a house. We have already traveled to destinations I had previously only dreamed of and we continue to enhance each others' lives on a daily basis. I am ready for the next adventure and whatever it brings.

Life Lab Lessons

- What have you learned from the various phases of your life?
- What do you treasure most?
- What would you have done differently?

- Are you happy with how you are dealing with your current circumstances?

- Are you ready for whatever awaits you in the future?

Chapter 3

The Powers of Man

We have many powers at our disposal. I don't think we are often aware of them. While there may be more, Charles Fillmore lists twelve. Here are reflections on a number of them I would like to share with you. Always do your best to use them as wisely as you possibly can

*****

The Power of Will

We look forward to the time when the Power of Love will replace the Love of Power. Then will our world know the blessings of peace.

~William Ewart Gladstone~

Thy will be done. The will of the people. Last will and testament. Will is an important concept running through our religion, politics and final bequests. I wonder how many of us have ever stopped to ponder its power and meaning. I know I haven't until recently.

To my mind will is a mental force of determination. Sometimes it refers to what we think God wants us to do. Sometimes it refers to our collective beliefs as a nation and sometimes it refers to what we as individuals want to have happen. Of course there are many other meanings as well.

These wills do not always coexist peacefully. Religious texts and government documents sometimes conflict in their expectations of how we should act. Sometimes our desires as individuals lie in direct conflict with religious or government expectations.

Without trying to resolve the problems of the universe in a single article, I would like to address individual will which can be consistent or volatile. The dictionary defines volatile as "lively, changing quickly or easily from one mood or interest to another."

Sometimes what we want remains fairly consistent. We can be very determined when our basic needs or wants are threatened. Our will can also be volatile depending on the situation and context. We can be at peace when our wishes coincide with the wishes of those around us. We can become irate when others contradict our wishes. A third possibility is being at war with ourselves when we try to honor conflicting internal values.

Where does our will originate? Sometimes we want what our parents wanted. Sometimes we want the opposite. Sometimes our experiences forge our will. A person raised in poverty might do anything to avoid re-experiencing it. A person raised without love might sacrifice everything else to feel loved. A person with treasured possessions might fight to the death to protect them.

Our greatest challenge may be how to balance our wills with those of the people around us. In my experience, it is not possible for us to have everything we want and at the same time allow others to have whatever they want. Our needs will at least occasionally clash, sometimes to the core of our beings.

So what should we do? I think the keys are cooperation and compromise. First we must understand what other people want. Sometimes what sounds like a conflict might be just a matter of semantics. We might both want the same thing but express it in different words.

The other part is compromise. Knowing we can't have everything we want if others are also to have their way, we need to determine what we hold most dear and understand the same about other people. Then we can find a way to negotiate ways for everyone to have at least part of what they want.

Life Lab Lessons

- List your most important values.

- List the values of those with whom you are in conflict.

- If you don't know what is important to them, ask.

- Decide which of your values are negotiable.

- Negotiate.

The Power of Strength

Greatness lies not in being strong, but in the right use of strength.

~Henry Ward Beecher~

Strength is a physical characteristic which can be used for good and bad. We can use it to accomplish important tasks when needed. Building houses, growing food and even getting from one place to another call on our physical strength. Fighting off attacks requires us to be strong. Protecting ourselves and those we love can also call on our strength.

Sometimes we use our power for less noble purposes. Bullies grab what they want from weaker people. Other people use their speed to reach what they want before others can get there.

Strength is also mental. We can use our thinking to determine how to handle difficult problems. We can learn to handle threats by avoiding them rather than direct confrontation. We can also consider alternate ways of doing something to see which way might be best.

Our minds might also pursue devious purposes. Examples are tricking people into doing what we want while disregarding their best interests lying to others to get what we want and lying to ourselves to justify what we do.

We also have spiritual assurances that what we do in life has a higher purpose. Our long term goals take us beyond immediate difficulties. But our power of choice can ignore what we believe and act only in our own best interests, setting aside what we have learned about God, nature and humanity.

A family life of deprivation and abuse can incline us to seek revenge on people we see as having offended us. If we can't get back at them, we might be tempted to take out our anger on whoever is available.

A supportive and peaceful family life can incline us to share our good fortune with others physically, mentally and spiritually. We would like others to find the peace we have found for ourselves.

Despite our backgrounds, life experiences and goals always have choices before us. We can choose to be selfish or concerned about others, greedy or generous, mean or kind, warlike or peaceful. Every time we make choices, what we choose becomes part of us.

As Charles Fillmore put it, "We grow to be like that which we idealize." People don't become saints or monsters by single acts. What we think about, wish for and choose on a daily basis moves us toward a certain way of being. How do we want to live our lives and how do we want others to see us?

Life Lab Lessons

- Think about the physical, mental and spiritual power you have.
- How do you use your power?
- What is really important to you?
- Are you moving in a life direction you find worthwhile?
- If not, what could you change?

The Power of Faith

I meditate and pray all the time.
The faith and respect that I have in the power of God in my life
is what I've used to keep myself grounded and it has allowed me
to move away from the storms that were in my life. I'm still a

work in progress,
but I know that as long as I stay close to God I'll be all right.

~Halle Berry~

At one time, most everyone could agree that faith was a good thing. It meant comfort, direction and support for our life struggles. In recent times, the very word has become divisive. Some of us believe we know the right way and others are wrong or confused. The struggle over "true religion" has been waged for centuries with attempts to obliterate one or another sect, depending on the century.

I remember reading a book by Jon Krakauer called *Under the Banner of Heaven.* One of the characters, a radical Mormon, claimed to have received a revelation from God saying he should kill his sister in law who opposed his polygamy. He killed his infant niece as part of the bargain.

Of course, faith is not all bad. It has brought meaning to many who struggle for a sense of meaning for their lives. Faith has given people a higher purpose as well as a context for their actions. Living a life of faith has taken people beyond their own immediate needs and helped them to see the purpose of sacrificing some of their own good for God and their fellow creatures.

I have heard faith defined as "the evidence for things unseen." In that sense, faith differs from common sense or science. It is a different way of knowing from using our senses or logic. Many writers have held that faith is the basis for science since any scientific exploration starts with certain assumptions.

Religious faith means belief in God. Some people hold that the existence of God can be proven by natural means. The reality is that once we start with the assumption that God exists, what we observe in nature confirms our belief.

So what power does faith have? It has power over our lives to direct us in a more selfless direction. It brings people together for a higher purpose. It gives us a spiritual goal for our lives. It keeps us from grabbing what we can from life without regard for anyone else.

Karen Armstrong, in her book, *The Battle for God*, talks about fundamentalists of various religions. She describes them as motivated by "militant piety." It is their job to convert or destroy anyone who does not hold with their way of thinking. They usually want to bring society under the control of those who think the way they do.

We seem to have become mired in a conflict between secular and religious ways of viewing the world and our lives. It is often difficult to reconcile what we see and what we believe. I think the challenge for all of us is to be humble, admitting that we are not perfect and all-knowing. We also need to accept that those who disagree with us are also seeking the best way to live their lives. Somehow we need to learn to listen to each other.

Life Lab Lessons

- Does what you believe show in what you do on a daily basis?

- Hear what is important to other people.

- Look for agreements between your beliefs and those of others.

- Offer your wisdom to others rather than trying to impose it.

- Look at everyone else as a fellow life traveler.

The Power of Imagination

It is the marriage of the soul with Nature
that makes the intellect fruitful, and gives birth to imagination.

~Henry David Thoreau~

Did you ever arise in the morning thinking about what faced you and then plodded through the rest of the day? If you allow yourself to, you can become an automaton. Many adults do it. Maybe that is why we have road rage and surliness in our daily life experience. Do you remember when you were a child and woke up wondering what adventures awaited you that day? Just because we are adults does not mean we have to jump on a treadmill rather than using our imaginations.

It seems hard for most of us to find a balance. Some of us rigidly plod along the path we think is expected of us, doing our duty but giving no thought to how we could enjoy the journey. Others are dreamers, following our flights of fancy but sometimes not tending to our obligations. Sometimes we follow a course set for us by others without thinking. Sometimes we stop to set our own course. Reaching a compromise between duty and imagination isn't easy.

Is there a middle ground? Maybe there doesn't have to be one for everybody. There is room in the world for its dreamers, plodders and everyone in between. Some of us become famous artists, learning how to portray our universe in a way which allows the rest of us a fresh perspective. Others see it as their duty to do the things which have to be done so that others can be free to do what they want to do. My Uncle Bob took the latter course, but did so cheerfully.

How do we compromise between duty and imagination? One way would be to divide our time between meeting our responsibilities and having fun. Many people take this approach. Still there are others who always bring their work home with them and yet others who never get serious.

Another way to approach the issue is to find creative ways to do what needs doing. Meeting our expectations in a joyless manner is not much fun. Consider Ebenezer Scrooge in Dickens' *A Christmas Carol* and what his day was like. Even worse were his times of solitude after work. Then consider Owen Meany in John Irving's novel *A Prayer for Owen Meany*. Owen lived a very creative and fascinating life despite many serious limitations.

Although these writings offer examples of extremes, we all have the choice to put some creativity into our everyday tasks, or adventures if we choose to look at them as such. What it takes is imagination. Rather than approaching something tediously and looking forward to the end of our task, we can ask ourselves the question "What if...?" and let our imaginations wander to ways in which our obligations can become adventures.

Life Lab Lessons

- Decide what is the most boring part of your life?

- Imagine ways you can make it more interesting.

- List the tasks you most dread.

- Think about how you could make them adventures.

- Invite others to help you make your relationships more interesting.

The Power of Love

Love is by nature exceedingly timid and modest,
but when roused-bold and fearless in the extreme.

~Charles Fillmore~

There is probably more written about love than any other topic. Love is the opposite of conflict and hatred and has many meanings. We think of love as a romantic feeling, warm and fuzzy, which draws us to another person. It has no reason or explanation. It's just how we feel. We can't explain it although people have tried in various ways over the centuries.

Love can also mean sexual desire. Love and sexuality can be intertwined in a relationship and complement each other. But it is also possible to love someone without being sexually attracted and to be sexually attracted to someone we don't love. The two are often confused. Sometimes one partner is motivated chiefly by love and the other by passion.

Love can mean caring for someone. We can wish the best for someone and do what we can to make his or her life better. Sometimes we sacrifice our own needs for the sake of the person we love. The degree of our love for that person determines how much we are willing to sacrifice.

Sometimes our love is not returned. It can be very lonely and disappointing to continue loving a person who does not return our love. Sometimes it is returned and we bond in a life of mutual caring. It is certainly much more satisfying to love a person when our love is returned.

We sometimes use love to mean we like a thing or an activity. My children had a standard joke in reply to my saying I loved something, "If you love it, why don't you marry it?" Love can be silly at times. Love for things is not the same as love for a person. Things don't love us back. There is nothing personal in this love. It is just a matter of enjoyment.

We also talk of God's love for us, love of our family members, our friends and our fellow beings in the abstract. Love can obviously mean many things. For me there are two basic meanings. One is how we feel about someone and the other is what we do about it.

There are many different levels of feeling love. They range from temporary good feelings to lifelong commitment and devotion. There are also many different levels of response to love. We might not do anything at all other than enjoy the good feeling. We might show our caring for another person when it is convenient. We might also put that person's needs and desires before our own.

Simon and Garfunkel sang "I am a rock; I am an island." John Donne wrote, "No man is an island." Where do you fit?

Life Lab Lessons

- What does love mean to you?
- Who loves you and why?
- What is the best thing about being loved?
- Whom do you love and why?
- What is the best thing about loving someone?

Joseph G. Langen

The Power of Order

Dream as if you'll live forever, live as if you'll die today.

~James Dean~

Order in the universe is cited as one of the natural proofs for the existence of God. "Clean up your room and get it in order before your father comes home!" Most of the time we like things to be orderly. How much time would we spend looking for our keys if we left them in a different place each time we came in the house? What would it be like to be expected at work a different time each day? For that matter, what would our lives be like if the seasons of the year were random rather than predictable?

We expect people to drive on the same side of the road all the time. We expect streets to have the same names each day unless we drove in Boston during the Big Dig. We expect to see cars driving on the road and people walking on sidewalks.

We are so dependent on order in our lives that we don't often stop to think about what it would be like if the rules for work, home life and sports changed every day. We can be disoriented by a football game with Australian rules or attending a European football game only to find teams playing what looks suspiciously like soccer.

Order helps us make sense of our lives and know what to expect. Without it we would feel as puzzled about our daily adventures as Alice in Wonderland. We feel like Brer Rabbit when people don't respond to our greetings as we expect them to. Not only do we appreciate order in our lives, we are downright annoyed when we don't find it. Zip-a-de-do-dah.

But is order always paramount? Just because things have been one way for a long time doesn't mean they should stay that way. Slavery was once seen as a normal state of affairs. So were persecuting people with different religious beliefs. Civil rights have not always been taken for granted.

Progress has often been slowed by our traditional beliefs. For centuries hardly anyone could conceive of riding in a self propelled machine, flying from one place to the other or walking on the moon. Often our imaginations are in conflict with the way we "know" things will always be.

So when is order helpful and when is it a hindrance? Order is helpful to us in those parts of our lives where we are comfortable on automatic pilot, the times when we don't have to stop to think about what we are doing. Order gets in our way when our habits create problems for us and for others, making our lives more difficult. Maybe it would help to think about our routines once in a while to see if they still make sense.

Life Lab Lessons

- Think about what parts of your life you like the way they are.

- What do you do that others count on?

- What habits get you in trouble on a regular basis?

- What could you do differently?

- Are you willing to experiment?

The Power of Understanding

To know someone here or there
with whom you can feel there is understanding
in spite of distances or thoughts expressed.
That can make life a garden.

~Goethe~

Sometimes I stop to wonder why there are so many divorces, fights, arguments and hard feelings among people. I think I have finally found one of the culprits- mind reading.

You might think of the magic trick where the magician figures out what card you have chosen. Possibly you imagine an old married couple one of whom anticipates what the other is about to say. Or maybe you invite a friend over for dinner and serve exactly what your friend had imagined.

I was sitting on my porch with the above words on my pad, trying to decide what to write next. Along came my mailwoman, Jen, who asked what I was writing as she delivered my mail. After I told her, she offered her opinion that too often people are caught up in their own thoughts and don't empathize with others. They make up their own minds rather than walking a mile in someone else's shoes. Could she have been mindreading and known exactly what thought I needed next? I suppose so.

When I sat in counseling with warring couples, I frequently pointed out their pattern of mind reading. They spoke as if they were in each other's heads or acted as if the other person said something they hadn't.

I suppose mind reading is harmless enough if you don't go off half cocked and react to something that might or might not be true. What if you decide your spouse, child, parent or friend is deliberately trying to be obnoxious and do something rotten in return? You might have just started a needless battle which could rage for years. And it could all be due to your faulty imagination and your mind reading.

So how do you get to understand someone? Even if they are talking the same language, people sometimes mean different things by the same words, glances, or mannerisms. Sometimes a person has no idea what another means and assumes that everyone means the same thing by what they say or do. They don't.

One way to understand people is to ask, "Is what you mean?" Isn't that better than assuming you know and fly off the handle in response? You could tell people how you feel when they say or do something which upsets you. When you talk about your feelings rather than attacking others, you have a much better chance of them hearing you. There are no doubt other alternatives as well. Mind reading can be fun when it is a game but devastating when serious matters are at stake.

Life Lab Lessons

- Think of any unresolved issues you have with people. Could they be due to misunderstandings?

- What could you do to resolve the matter?

- Have you ever been surprised when someone got upset about something you said or did when you meant no harm?

- If there are still hard feelings about it, would it help if you explain what you meant?

- If you are locked in conflict with someone, try stopping to listen to each other's position rather than just insisting you are right.

Joseph G. Langen

Chapter 4

Making Sense of Society

We don't live in a vacuum. While society complicates our lives, it also makes them more interesting. We don't always accept the rules of our society and sometimes feel the need to challenge them. Regardless of how we react to them, it's good to know what the rules are and where they came from so we better decide what to do about them.

*****

Living in Our World Community

Hear me, four quarters of the world - a relative I am! Give me the strength to walk the soft earth, a relative to all that is! Give me the eyes to see and the strength to understand, that I may be like you. With your power only can I face the winds.

~Black Elk~

I have been reading Eckhart Tolle lately and thinking about his call for a higher consciousness rather than being trapped by our thinking. His words reminded me of the writings of Teilhard de Chardin, a French priest who wrote about cosmic consciousness and Thomas Berry, a priest I knew in the 1960's who wrote about awareness of being connected with the rest of creation.

It seems hard for us to think of ourselves as a world community. Many people disparage the United Nations as useless. Society is pitted Republican versus Democrat, Christian versus Moslem, Jew versus Palestinian, radical religious thinker versus secular thinker. The list goes on. It feels to me like the whole world has taken sides on just about every conceivable issue. We can't even agree on the earth. Some people think we are in danger of destroying our habitat while others think the idea of global warming is nonsense.

Despite differences in how we look or act, we all have a great deal in common with each other even in our physical makeup. We come from the earth when we are born and will return to it when we die. In the mean time we interact with the earth every time we eat, drink or draw a breath. We are all part of the same earth. It's hard to be any more connected to the earth and to each other than that.

There should be some way we can treat each other as part of the same community. I have been thinking about such a development and waiting for it for the past forty years. The reality is that it won't happen by itself. We must all do our part to bring about such a change.

How? Of course none of us can change the whole world all by ourselves. None of us has control of anyone else's interactions with their world neighbors. What we can do is to start treating every person we meet as a cherished member of our world community.

Life Lab Lessons

- Start thinking of others as part of your world community.

- Make them feel welcome in your world.

- Start with people you fine easiest to welcome.

- As you progress, work up to people harder for you to welcome.

- See if you can have a relationship with someone and leave out all the labels we use to categorize people.

Raising the World Family

What a cruel thing is war: to separate and destroy families and friends, and mar the purest joys and happiness God has granted us in this world; to fill our hearts with hatred instead of love for our neighbors, and to devastate the fair face of this beautiful world.

~Robert E. Lee~

Violence seems to be increasing, especially in Iraq. Although opinions about the reasons abound, the violence continues and worsens on an almost daily basis. We tend to argue with each other as a nation about whose fault it is and what to do about it. Sometimes it seems hopeless. Thinking about the whole world is not easy and seems overwhelming. Could we look at things on a somewhat smaller scale?

What about the family? What does it take to raise responsible children? First we must look at our attitude about ourselves. Some parents consider themselves demagogues, the ultimate authority and rulers of their families. They are often heard saying "Because I said so" when their children question their decisions. Some parents think respect is a one way street, their children's responsibility but not theirs. Some parents do not seem to realize that their children learn more from how they see their parents live their lives than from what parents preach to their children.

Children are not soldiers and cannot be expected to follow their parents' expectations and demands without question. Although they might do so at first, part of growing up is learning to think for themselves. As they grow older, children question their parents' expectations and ways of doing things. They will eventually learn to make their own decisions. They might adopt their parents' ways, adopt opposite ways of acting or find a compromise, accepting some of their parents' ideas and rejecting others. Although parents often wish their children could be spared their own mistakes, it does not always happen. Children tend to make their own mistakes and hopefully learn from them.

What can parents do? The first thing is to help their children understand why they have the rules they do. They need to help their children understand the consequences of their actions and that whatever people do has good or bad consequences for them as well as for others.

Treating their children as valuable persons helps them see others' value as they grow up. Children can learn respect but are not likely to initiate it unless they are shown how. Children learn from example. The best way for parents to teach them to make wise choices is to set an example in their own lives. They should also explain their choices to their children so they don't have to learn everything on their own by trial and error.

What does this have to do with the world? It has been said that all politics are local. It is also true that all relationships are personal. How we deal with each other on a daily basis affects the relationships of everyone we meet. We can also set an example for each other of how to live responsibly and how to respect each other.

Life Lab Lessons

- If you are having a conflict with your child, try listening first to their point of view and then sharing yours.

- Stop to think what a stranger's life might be like.

- If someone is struggling, think about what you could do to help.

- Think about other civilizations as neighbors rather than strangers.

- Act toward others as you would like them to act toward you.

Keeping Law and Order in Balance

Only the man who has enough good in him
to feel the justice of the penalty can be punished.

~William Ernest Hocking~

I grew up feeling suffocated. My father had too many rules which often did not make sense to me. I spent quite a bit of time trying to dodge them, sometimes outright ignoring them at my peril. As an adult, I have not been much of a proponent of rules either and have preferred to set my own course whenever I can. I prefer to work independently than for someone else.

Rules are hard to escape. Christians have the Ten Commandments. Jews have the Torah as well. Muslims have the Koran. Followers of other beliefs have their own prescriptions and proscriptions. Citizens of countries have laws and constitutions. Residents of municipalities have ordinances. Even if we live in caves, we have natural law. Our universe is one of laws whether we like it or not.

We can choose to defy or ignore any of these laws. However we must also be prepared for the consequences whether from church, government or nature itself. Did you ever decide you did not agree with the law of gravity and could jump off a cliff without falling to the ground? I thought not.

Over the years, I have come to accept rules and laws as ways to help us know what to expect of each other. They help proceed with the business of life without having to figure out each social situation we face. They also tell us what rights and obligations each of us has and what happens if we ignore them.

Unfortunately legal systems do not always protect us. Laws have sometimes been adopted by those in power for their own benefit and have been used to persecute those who get in their way. Although it is hard to argue with the laws of nature, some religions have decided what constitutes "natural law" and tried to impose their interpretation on the rest of us.

Although our civilization would be chaotic without any rules, we need to balance them with common sense. Thomas Paine wrote about this at the time of our country's founding: "…a long habit of not thinking a thing wrong, gives it a superficial appearance of being right, and raises at first a formidable outcry in defense of custom." We can take our laws for granted and assume they represent the way things should be. Slavery was legal in our country for many years.

So what should we do? I think we should return to the cracker barrel discussion and refine our opinions rather than having them fed to us by television. We don't often take time to listen to each other and sometimes follow the example of our national leaders as they try to upstage each other, promoting their own agendas to the detriment of the rest of us. What do you think?

Life Lab Lessons

- Reflect on what is most important to you in life.
- Find out what is important to other people you know or even meet by chance.
- Think about customs you take for granted.
- Do they mean the same to others as they do to you?
- Think about how you could change your routine to improve life for others around you.

Walking in the Shoes of Another

What else is love but understanding and rejoicing in the fact that another person lives, acts and experiences otherwise than we do?

~Friedrich Nietzsche~

Why is it so easy to become locked in conflict with a spouse, child, friend, or colleague? Why is it even easier to lock horns with a stranger? I don't think most of us go around looking for a fight although a few of us do. Most of us would prefer to live in peace with others. Yet many times it doesn't happen. Are others waiting for us to come along so they can have a good fight? Probably not.

Then what's the problem? I think it boils down to not knowing what it feels like to be someone else. We tend to view others based on how we think and act. We judge others' behavior based on what it would mean if we acted the way they did. We are upset because others do not think, feel and act as we do. Put that way, it doesn't sound quite fair, does it? If we look at our own actions, I think most of us would agree that there have been times when we have acted in ways which horrify or at least surprise others. We assume it is up to others to understand us. If they knew what was in our mind, our actions should make perfect sense to them.

How often do we stop to understand others' points of view? Most of us tend to mind-read. We assume we know what others are thinking, what is important to them and why they do what they do. Where do we get these ideas? Sometimes we imagine what we would do in their situation. Sometimes we assume they are just like others we have seen act the same way in the past. Sometimes we decide they must know better and are just acting stupid.

None of these assumptions is helpful in understanding others. Attacking them or rejecting them because of what we assume about their thoughts, feelings and motives is not helpful either. So what can we do? There is an old saying, probably of Native American origin, saying never to criticize a person until we have walked a mile in his, or her, moccasins. It is not possible to live another person's life. Our experience would be different given others' circumstances.

There are ways to understand someone else's experience. We can observe that person for a while, ask others what they know of the person or gently ask about his or her life. The key is to put aside our judgments and ask questions with true interest. If someone takes an unbiased interest in our lives, I think most of us are fairly likely to explain ourselves, assuming we have some understanding of our own actions. Otherwise, we might be more prone to figure out why we act the way we do.

Life Lab Lessons

- Work on recognizing when you are being judgmental.
- Try to put aside your judgment and be more objective.
- Create an opportunity for others to share with you how they experience life.
- Listen without judging.
- See how your experience matches that of others.

Is It Worth Being Polite?

Many who would not take the last cookie
would take the last lifeboat.

~Mignon McLaughlin~

Being polite may seem trite. I am sure we all remember our parents asking, "Now what do you say?" if a please or thank you was required. There was also the mild embarrassment of needing to be reminded.

Does it really matter if we show good manners? Do others get anything out of it? Do we? Is it worth the extra effort? Think about the choices we have in social situations. Take for example buying a cup of coffee at a restaurant. We can be perfunctory and just say thanks. We can go beyond this and complement the clerk on their quick service or sunny disposition. We can complete the transaction without any comment or gesture. We can also find something to complain about or throw our money on the counter rather than handing it to the clerk directly.

The answer to the question above is yes, it does matter. Everything we say, do or don't do has an effect both on the other person and on ourselves. The consequences of a brief interaction may not be profound but they do exist.

There are several implications for the other person. If we complete the transaction in a totally neutral way with no meaningful comments or gestures, we are treating the other person as a machine with no feelings.

If we are critical or nasty in our comments or mannerisms, the other person will see us as threatening. We may be upset about something totally unrelated, but attacking the other person will only leave them feeling defensive or angry.

We can also be pleasant, find something to compliment, or find a pleasant way to convey any concerns we have without framing them as an attack.

Whether or not we are polite also has implications for us. If we are completely neutral in our interactions, we act less than human as well as treating the other person mechanically.

If we are critical or nasty, we move a little closer each time to viewing the world as hostile. Every negative interaction takes us further into an attitude of belligerence toward everyone else. At a very basic level a warlike attitude also has negative effects on our blood pressure and other aspects of our physical well being.

If we are polite, even in conveying our concerns, we will have an easier time staying at peace with ourselves, feel better about those we meet during the course of the day and keep our bodies tuned as a side benefit.

Of course, we don't have control over how the rest of the world acts. Another thing I remember my mother saying was, "It's up to you to set a good example." We can do this for everyone we meet. Although our example might not change them radically, it might give them something to think about. We started out talking about a minor example of buying a cup of coffee. What if we took our polite manners with us into more important interactions as well?

Life Lab Lessons

- How important is politeness to you?
- Are people polite to you?
- Are you polite to others?
- Do people treat to you the way you treat them?
- Maybe your example can influence how people treat each other.

Names Will Never Hurt Me

It is best to live from your heart
and speak from your heart in all things
yet, if you cannot always speak from your heart,
live from your heart and let the speaking come in time.

~Laura Teresa Marquez~

Remember the childhood saying, "Sticks and stones will break my bones, but names will never hurt me?" A brave defense, but usually not very successful. Most people do more damage with their words than with their fists or weapons. Words don't leave visible marks but what we say to others can leave them feeling ashamed, embarrassed or enraged.

I remember attending high school in a seminary out of town. One of my classmates decided to start calling me "Chester" since I was from Rochester. I was somewhat overweight and had larger breasts than most of my classmates. The same classmate took to calling me "Chesty" or "Breasty" when he was in a particularly nasty mood. I could have made up a nick name based on his last name, but it was too frankly sexual. I might have been able to beat him up, but outright violence was definitely frowned on in the seminary. As it was, I frequently felt humiliated and self conscious. Names and comments can certainly hurt us.

I dare say none of us would relish being called names or being the subject of gossip or rumor. Before you engage in destructive speech, think back to a time when you were the recipient of such a verbal attack. You are about to engender in your target the same feelings which once plagued you. Is it worth it? Speaking of worth, how do you know if something is worth saying? There is a three-fold test.

First, is what you are about to say true? Have you observed first-hand what you are about to say? We have no way of knowing whether gossip is true. I remember a classroom experiment in which the teacher whispered something to one student and told him to whisper what he heard to the next student and so on. By the time the last student whispered to the teacher, what she said bore no resemblance to the original statement. Even something that starts as true has a strong chance of being distorted as it passes through the rumor mill.

Second, is it kind? Will what you say make the subject of your statement feel any better? Will it improve the quality of his or her life? Repeating gossip is not a kind thing to do. Gossip poisons the network of people we hear it from and pass it on to. In the process, we poison our own thinking and tip the balance of our thoughts a little more toward the negative. We become a little more bitter-tongued each time.

Third, is it purposeful? What is the point of what we say? Do our words contribute anything positive? Gossip is usually a way to make us feel better. We find faults in others we don't want to see in ourselves. Even if we know something bad to be true of someone, we would accomplish more by offering sympathy or assistance to the victim of gossip, if we think it would be well received.

Another option in the face of gossip would be to say we would rather not discuss things we know nothing about. We can also pass back something good we have heard about the person in question. We have a choice of what we listen to and a choice of what we say. Choosing wisely will make the world a better place a little at a time.

Life Lab Lessons

- As a child did anyone give you a hated nickname?
- How did it make you feel?
- Have you ever seen you words hurt someone?
- Was it worth it?
- How can you use what you say more constructively?

What Respect Has To Do With Violence

When you are content to be simply yourself and don't compare or compete, everybody will respect you.

~Lao-Tzu~

I once wrote about an incident of inner city violence. A young man felt that someone was looking at his girlfriend in a way which did not appear respectful to him. Was that just his feeling or is there a connection between respect and violence?

John Lampman wrote in the *Christian Science Monitor* in February, 2006 about violence as being rooted in disrespect, leading to feelings of shame and humiliation, resulting in people feeling inferior, or at least as if they are viewed that way by others. If a person does not feel good about himself or herself to start with, he or she often feels there is nothing to lose and sometimes lashes out in violence.

Violence is a tactic some people use to seek recognition by others and in some way remind us that they have some power. It usually doesn't work, and we end up disparaging the person further, leading to more shame and humiliation and eventually more violence. The cycle of disrespect and violence tends to self-perpetuate.

Why are some people more likely to react to perceived disrespect than others? Think what it would be like to be born into a poor family and see others around you with plenty while your family lacks the basic necessities. Imagine having parents who don't think much of themselves and pass on to you their lack of self confidence. What if your parents resented you for even being alive or look down on a disability or shortcoming you have through no fault of your own?

Imagine your teachers making fun of your limitations or resenting your efforts to think for yourself. What if other students take up your teacher's disrespect and make your life a constant torture? What if you have a hard time finding a good job and being able to take care of your own needs not to mention those of your family?

All of these experiences can lead you to feel shame about who you are, embarrassed about being seen in public and helpless to do anything about your situation. As a result you become angry and frustrated. Since you already see others as not having much use for you, you might just as well show your anger and lash out at others. What have you got to lose?

One answer is for those more fortunate to find ways to respect those less fortunate. We can listen to what it is like for others rather than dismissing them as worthless. We can offer our help to get them started in a new direction if they ask for it. We can address our differences, starting with understand them before telling them what we think. We can make a difference but we must start with knowing what others are about and seeing how we can work together.

Life Lab Lessons:

- Start by understanding your own strengths and weaknesses.

- Think about what traits of yours make you feel less worthy.

- Start working on what you can change about yourself.

- If you are stuck, think about who you could ask for help.

- After you work on yourself, try harder to understand others, especially those who differ from you.

What to Do If You Get No Respect

Respect cannot be learned, purchased or acquired- it can only be earned.

~Bits and Pieces~

When I worked at a day treatment center for delinquent boys in Philadelphia, the words "Yo' Mama" were enough to provoke a fist fight or worse. Outside the inner city, people have more subtle ways of reacting to feeling disrespected: road rage, tailgating, being surly with store employees, writing nasty letters to the editor. I think people sometimes act this way because they feel they are due respect which is not forthcoming.

As a psychologist, I have worked with parents, usually fathers, who demand "respect" from their children while at the same time treating them with disrespect. "I'm the parent!" Psychologists call this a sense of entitlement, a feeling that one is owed something.

So why is respect so important to many people? Some grow up in families where they were treated as valuable and worthwhile. Their parents listened to their fears, interests and desires and took them seriously. Products of such families don't usually have an issue with respect. What if your parents treated you as a bother, didn't care about your feelings and thought only of their own needs and desires? Respect is a two way street, but parents can't expect their children to make the first move. It is up to parents to show their children how to be respectful.

I don't think the problem with respect is entirely the fault of parents. I'm not sure whose fault it is or how we got this way as a culture. We have been very blessed in our country in many ways. Our lifestyle is more comfortable than that of people in many other countries. It seems to me that we take for granted what we have and see our well-being as our birthright. Any inconvenience in our daily life seems like an imposition and outrages or at least annoys us. We deserve what we have and then some. The American dream is to grab all we can in our journey through life. We want a little more, even if it means others must make do with a little less.

There is another side to our way of life. We have a history of coming to the aid of those who need help, protecting those who can't fend for themselves and making room for other cultures while they assimilate into our way of life. There are many who have gone out of their way to help others throughout our history. Maybe we learned from the example of native peoples who helped our early settlers through the first difficult winters.

You can't go back to your childhood and choose parents who respect themselves and who will respect you and then grow up again. You can practice being grateful for your good traits and whatever measure of good fortune comes your way. You can learn to respect others by giving them a chance to share their fears, hopes and dreams. Understanding is the first step. You can also show your children how to respect others by valuing them and by your example in how you approach everyone you meet.

Life Lab Lessons

- Make a list of all the wonderful things about you.

- List all the blessings you have in your life.

- Tell your spouse and children what is wonderful about them.

- Look first for the goodness in people you meet.

- If you find yourself being critical, read over the above lists.

Of Jesus, Priests and Gays

*Any fool can criticize, condemn, and complain but it takes
character and self control to be understanding and forgiving.*

~Dale Carnegie~

I recently noticed that the major headlines and most of the
newspaper columns focused on the movie The Passion of the
Christ, priest molesters and gay marriage. They all had themes
centering on whether people should be exposed to the violence
of Jesus' Passion, the offending priests and the "marriage
undermining" gays. Not much effort was expended to make
sense of the issues involved. They all discussed what to do about
the various issues without seeking to understand them.

Most anyone who has heard of Jesus is familiar with the story of
his torture and crucifixion. It would be hard not to be aware of
recent news about sexual abuse perpetrated by priests or of gay
and lesbian marriages.

Discussion of the movie The Passion of the Christ has focused
on potential reaction to the violence it portrays, especially when
viewed by children. Movie violence has been decried for years
as harmful to children, although this movie is seen as a possible
exception.

Discussion of priest molesters has focused on identifying and
weeding out the offending priests. A zero tolerance policy is
emerging, leading to isolation of them from their ministry and
prohibiting them from performing priestly duties.

Discussion of gay marriage has focused on gays undermining
traditional marriage, which many see as primarily a sacred
ground for raising children. There is no reference to the many
heterosexual marriages which don't last, or people who marry
after their childbearing years. It is as if gays are less serious
about their commitment to their relationships and are mocking
the institution of marriage.

We seem to have stopped thinking about things in our culture
and are instead reacting to events emotionally. If people make us
uncomfortable, let's get rid of them or get them out of our
awareness.

Joseph G. Langen

I have not seen anything written about how a significant number of priests, committed to celibacy, could do such things to children. What is it about them or about our culture which led to this pattern?

I have not heard much discussion of why gay people want to get married. Could they want to profess their love for each other as straight people do? Could they also be concerned about stability and security in their lives? What about gays who marry with concern about the well-being of their children?

What would Jesus have to say about these issues? He was horrified by the thought of his own death. He taught that we should love each other as God has loved us. I don't remember any exceptions. He also spent a fair amount of time engaged with others who had been shunned by society.

Maybe it is time we start trying to understand those who make us uncomfortable rather than shoving them aside and getting them out of our sight. It is not our role to judge others. "Let the one who is without sin cast the first stone." ~John 8:7~

Life Lab Lessons

- Do your opinions generate more heat or more light?
- Do you attack, defend or support others by your opinions?
- If you find your voice rising, what does the issue stir up in you?
- What are you afraid of?
- Think about whether you could change anything about yourself.

Turning the Tide from Conflict to Peace

*And into whatsoever house ye enter, first say, Peace be to this
house-
Pax huic domui et omnibus habitantibus in ea.*

~Luke, 10:5~

A number of years ago, I sang with the Genesee Chorale. We learned to sing settings of the Ave Maria which until then had been unknown to me. I was particularly surprised to learn that Stravinsky had arranged one. We also learned a variety of Christmas carols and motets. Thank you, Ted.

When the Christmas season arrived, we performed a concert in a church and also sang in the Genesee Country Mall. I don't know whether it was planned or a last minute thought, but we were invited to sing at a Christmas Eve celebration in a barn somewhere out by Pumpkin Hill.

It was a very cold night and I heard the muffled crackle of crusted snow beneath the new-fallen soft layer as I made my way from the car to the barn. The barn was lit only by candles. Two parents with a new baby reenacted the nativity scene. Various farm animals milled around, doing what animals have done for the past two thousand years. Somehow the animals knew enough to behave. In my mind they joined in our awe.

We sang our most spiritual hymns, leaving out Frosty and Santa Claus. I felt transported to the manger at Bethlehem. No matter what else was happening around us, this was a chance to think of the world renewed and with a chance of redemption. I did not know anyone else there other than my fellow Chorale members. However I felt a kinship with all present and knew they wished for me the peace I wished for them.

With all the turmoil, conflict and hatred in the world these days, I wonder whether it is possible to find a peaceful connection with others. I experienced it once in the barn and have had similar experiences with others at various times as well. So I know it is possible.

As I have watched the news, it has seemed to me that international conflict, distrust and downright hatred has filtered down into our communities and even into our personal relationships. Why can't our personal relationships filter back up to our local communities and ultimately to our national and international communities?

I think the message of Christmas, at least for me, is that the world can be transformed through our moments of inner peace and our willingness to share them with each other. The example of Baby Jesus in a manger with people taking time out to touch each other's lives tells me it is possible. Would you like to play your part?

Life Lab Lessons

- Find some time this Christmas to set aside your troubles at least for a while.

- Use this time to find a peaceful part of yourself and stay there awhile.

- Look for a way to share your peace with others you care about.

- Stretch yourself a little further and share your peace with strangers.

- Be open to how others' peace can touch your life.

Create Peace in Your Little Corner of the World

Think not forever of yourselves, O Chiefs, nor of your own generation. Think of continuing generations of our families, think of our grandchildren and of those yet unborn whose faces are coming from beneath the ground.

~T.S. Eliot~

Christmas is a time when we think of peace on earth and even sing about it. A gentle snowfall is peaceful. The earth and much of nature is still. Nevertheless we are surrounded by hostility, disagreement and armed conflict. Is thinking, praying or singing about peace enough?

We do not have magic wands to wave over the earth and its inhabitants to make everything peaceful. Bringing about peace seems too much for even the mightiest nations, much less single individuals. It all seems overwhelming. None of us can singlehandedly bring peace to the world or even to any significant portion of it.

What can we do? Fortunately, there are some alternatives at our disposal. Each of us lives in a little corner of the world, a space occupied by us and under our control. Others come and go throughout our lives, but our space is ours. We have some choices of how to arrange things in our little corner of the world.

We can put up a moat or barbed wire, making it difficult for anyone else to get in or out of our space. We can roar like lions to scare off anyone who approaches. We can discourage others with our quills, odor or poison. As another option, we can put out our welcome mat, sing and dance or write to attract others to spend some time with us.

Once others gain entrance to our space, we have the choice of how they will experience their visit with us. We can annoy them until they leave, argue with everything they say or just ignore them. We can also ask them about themselves, make an effort to understand them and take an interest in their lives.

Depending on how we treat them, visitors to our space can leave in a more hostile state than when they arrived. They can also leave in a more peaceful state, enriched by their visit to our space. Maybe we can't bring peace to the whole world at once by our individual efforts. But we can live in a peaceful space and offer some of our peace to those who visit us.

In order to share peace with others, we first must be at peace with ourselves. Did you ever stop to consider the wars raging within you and how they keep you from being at peace with others or with yourself for that matter? Most of us have some of these conflicts which keep us off balance. Maybe it is time to reach peace with ourselves and then practice sharing it with others.

Peace be with you and to all who dwell with you.

Life Lab Lessons

- In a moment of quiet, listen to your thoughts.

- Do you notice any arguments you are having with yourself?

- See if you can hear each side separately and clearly.

- What does each side want from you?

- How can you reconcile the conflicting positions within you?

Chapter 5

Understanding and Handling Feelings

Feelings can be very powerful. They can either help or hinder our efforts to live a good life. Did you ever think you were making a decision and later discover you acted entirely on your feelings? It helps to understand them and gain some perspective on how they affect our decisions. Anger seems to be a particularly troublesome emotion in our society.

*****

What on Earth is Emotional Intelligence?

Comparing the three domains, I found that for jobs of all kinds, emotional competencies were twice as prevalent among distinguishing competencies as were technical skills and purely cognitive abilities combined.

~Daniel Goleman~

Everybody wants smart kids. Nobody wants to be called dumb, ignorant or stupid. All these terms refer to what we know, or don't know, and how good we are at figuring things out. Most of the research on intelligence has focused on verbal, mechanical and mathematical abilities.

In the early 1900's, Alfred Binet developed a test to identify gifted students in the Paris schools. Many other tests have emerged since then to understand and classify levels of ability.

People can be viewed as "superior," "average" or "retarded" based on their IQ scores and other measures of ability. Where you fall on these measures helps get you into college or on disability.

None of the traditional intelligence tests measure how good we are at dealing with feelings or emotions. Emotional intelligence can be described as "the potential for learning self awareness, motivation, self regulation, empathy and adeptness in relationships and social skills."Emotional competence is the development of these abilities.

Why is emotional intelligence important?

When I first heard about emotional intelligence, I thought it might be just another fad. Then I discovered some interesting research. In one study following Harvard students in the years after graduation, higher traditional intelligence scores did not lead to higher salary, better job productivity or status, life satisfaction or happiness in relationships. Another study of teenagers in a neighborhood near Harvard found that childhood abilities to handle frustrations, control emotions and get along with other people made more of a difference in later life success than did traditional IQ.

What kind of feelings are we talking about?

People from various cultures have different names for emotions, including sadness, fear, enjoyment, love, surprise, disgust and shame. Research on facial expressions has found that people in most cultures can identify fear, anger, sadness and enjoyment from looking at pictures of people showing various emotions, suggesting that at least some emotions can be easily recognized across most all cultures.

What is the difference between emotional intelligence and emotional competence?

These two are a little different. Like most human abilities, people have more or less ability to deal with emotions. You can be born with a great deal of raw athletic talent but without training you will never be an athlete. Likewise, you can have very good potential to deal with emotions or emotional intelligence but will need training, experience or both to develop skills in handling emotions known as emotional competence. Peter Salovey has identified five areas of emotional competence.

- **Knowing your own emotions.**

The first competence is being able to recognize what you're feeling when you're feeling it and being able to put a name to it. For example, suppose you are usually quite patient with your children. One day you're driving them to a doctor's appointment and are afraid you will be late and need to reschedule the appointment. Your children start arguing over a toy while you are trying to get to the appointment on time. You bark at them rather than using your usual problem solving approaches. You realize that you're more upset than usual with your kids and you know the reason. This is an example of recognizing your feelings as they happen.

- **Managing your emotions.**

Someone else gets the promotion you expected. Do you respond with rage at your employer, think of ways to get revenge and undermine your competitor who got the promotion? Do you react with disappointment or ask for comfort from people who care about you? After you settle down you could meet with your boss to ask why the decision was made and what you can do to prepare for the next promotion opportunity. One way lets your emotions take over and weakens your standing at work. The other improves your status or at least lets you find out that you might be in the wrong job.

- **Motivating yourself**

You don't get what you want just by deciding you want to have it. There is usually a degree of effort involved that requires some determination. Sometimes there are obstacles to overcome or other people to convince that your goal is worthwhile. Whether or not you follow through with your decision depends on your level of motivation. Another way to put this is "How bad do you want it?" There certainly is a difference between feeling that it would be nice to pursue your goal and being determined to overcome any obstacle to reach it. The difference is your level of motivation.

- **Recognizing emotions in others**

This is not as simple as knowing that somebody else has feelings. People do not always come out and tell you directly what they are feeling. Sometimes they aren't quite sure of what they are feeling. Sometimes they might be embarrassed by certain feelings. Sometimes they might think you will not understand their feelings. People show how they feel in many ways other than using words. Becoming unusually loud, quiet, restless, withdrawn, glaring or avoiding eye contact are all nonverbal ways of expressing feelings. These cues might be a little difficult to read if you don't know the person well but can be important signs that something is going on in his or her world. Being alert to these changes can help you understand and react appropriately to another's feelings. Being aware of what someone is feeling can help you act in a way which will help that person do a better job at work, be a more loving partner or just be easier to live with. Knowing someone's feelings and doing something supportive will in the long run encourage others to react better to you and to your feelings.

- **Handling relationships**

If you understand another's emotions, you will be in a better position to get what you want. If you know that encouragement is important to your employees, how do you think they will react if you never comment when a report is done well or early, and instead just announce when the next project is due? Eventually they will become discouraged and conclude that it does not really matter to you how well a job they do and that you don't recognize extra effort. Other aspects of handling relationships include helping people work together and helping them to resolve conflicts. Your comments may cause two people to build barriers between themselves and to move from dislike to all out war. Your comments could also help them see that they both want the same thing or that each can get at least part of what they want through cooperation.

Thoughts vs. feelings

We are not talking about a war between thoughts and feelings or whether one is better than the other. Feelings can point us in the right direction when an important decision must be made. It is not just a question of what the "right" decision is, but what life will be like for you and for others when you make a particular decision. Let's look at two emotions and how they can shape our lives.

Anger

Suppose anger is the main theme of your life and influences how you react to everything that happens to you. Staying focused on your anger colors all the situations you find yourself in. You look for reasons to justify your anger and become increasingly angrier. Venting your anger used to be seen as a good way to get rid of it, letting off steam. It now seems that venting is not such a good idea. Venting your anger just keeps you in practice and makes it more likely that you will be angry the next time something happens that you don't like.

Anger is not always a bad or inappropriate response. But if you find yourself angry most of the time, there are some things you can do about it. Learning how to relax your body and your mind with approaches such as meditation can be helpful. Listening to and challenging your thoughts that lead to your anger also helps. Does your spouse leave the kitchen cabinets open just to annoy you or is he more likely just to be forgetful? Not everything people do is directed toward you. It is not always easy to learn relaxation and thought challenging techniques on your own. If you have trouble doing it on your own you might find counseling helpful.

Hope

Let's look at another emotion and how it might affect your life. Hope means believing that you have both the will and the way to accomplish your goals closely related to hope is optimism or a strong expectation that things will turn out all right despite setbacks and frustration. Optimists see failure as due to something that can be changed so that they can succeed next time. Pessimists react to setbacks by assuming there is nothing they can do to make things better.

While you may have inborn tendencies to be an optimist or a pessimist, you can also practice looking at things in a more optimistic way. Ask yourself; "What can I change so that I can be more successful next time?" Telling yourself you can be successful sounds corny but it works.

How do I Control My Emotions?

Emotions and feelings are not good or bad, but can be destructive at their extremes. We tend to think that we become upset by what happens in our lives. Somebody cuts us off in traffic and we react by becoming angry and blaring our horn.

Although this process seems simple, there is a little more to it. In between what happens and how we feel is what we tell ourselves about what happened. In the example of being cut off by another car, we may tell ourselves that the other driver is a clod who is only thinking of himself and has no regard for our rights to the road. What if we thought the other driver had a sick child in the back seat and was rushing the child to the hospital before the child dies? Would we feel the same as a result of this second train of thought? Not likely. Probably the best way to get our feelings under control is to start being aware of what we tell ourselves about the things that happen to us. We can challenge these ideas to see if they really make sense.

Emotions can be helpful in making decisions and in getting along with people. They can also be quite destructive. It is worth the investment to spend time becoming more aware of our own and others' feelings and putting both in perspective before reacting to situations.

Life Lab Lessons:

- Do you realize you can think about your emotions?
- How often are you aware of what you are feeling?
- How often are you aware of what others are feeling?
- Use this knowledge to understand what you and other people want.
- Work toward mutually satisfying outcomes.

Hope and Its Alternatives

When the world says, "Give up", Hope whispers, "Try it one more time."

~Author Unknown~

Hilary Clinton criticized her election opponent for offering voters false hope. I began to wonder whether my writing would be perceived as offering my readers false hope as well. In everything I write I try to help them see the effect of their thoughts and actions on others and realize that they have the option of acting in ways which will better themselves and maybe even the world community.

What are the alternatives to hope? As I see it, they consist of despair and rage. In the news, we see more dramatic suicides which to my mind indicate a growing level of despair in our society. We read almost weekly of equally dramatic killings which seem to be prompted by rage whether for religious, political or other reasons. We call those responsible sick or deeply troubled.

I'm not suggesting there is any easy answer to despair or rage. They don't seem to be related only to life circumstances. Some people living in what to us is squalor seem somehow content. Others of apparently good circumstance can become suicidal or homicidal. So where does hope fit in?

Hope alone is not enough. Hoping things will get better does not in itself bring about a betterment of our circumstances. But what if we mean by hope the possibility of life getting better? What if we act on that hope, start listening to each other and treating each other as valuable and important? Hope gives us the possibility and acting on it makes for a better world.

I remember many years ago reading Aesop's fable describing the argument between the Wind and the Sun about which was stronger. They decided on a contest to see which could get a man to remove his cloak. The Wind went first. The harder the Wind blew, the more tightly the man clutched his cloak. In turn, the Sun smiled in all its glory and off came the cloak. The moral was that we can get farther with kindness than with brute force. This fable has been a theme of my writing over the past few years.

I have seen the futility of rage and despair and have never seen either lead to an improvement in anyone's life situation. The more bitter a person becomes the more difficult life is and the harder it is to make it through each day and the easier it is to give up or lash out at someone. When something happens to bring us a ray of hope, life somehow seems again possible to manage. We might think we are being realistic instead of wallowing in negative emotions. But if our sense of realism includes not being able to do anything about our lives, we are still stuck.

Life Lab Lessons

- Is there anything in your life you think can never change?

- If this were a friend's problem instead of yours, what would you suggest?

- Even if you can see some options, do you think changing is too hard?

- Maybe you just haven't tried the right approach yet.

- If you're stuck, maybe you need to humble yourself and ask for help.

How I Learned to Take My Own Advice

The best way to succeed in life is to act on the advice we give to others.

~Author Unknown~

Several years ago I was struggling financially, emotionally and spiritually. It was all I could do to keep my soul alive and limping along from day to day. I had convinced myself that I faced a life of drudgery and that the best I would ever manage would be to survive. Would I spend the rest of my life bobbing in the ocean, clinging to bits of flotsam and jetsam from my former life?

At the time I was counseling a man stuck in a marriage that was essentially over. He had a hard time accepting its end and daring to take the next step. He also felt condemned to a life in tatters, with no prospects of putting it back together.

I worked with him until he was able to imagine coming back to life, take a few baby steps and eventually start to rebuild his life. I was glad I could support him, help him see what his choices were and be with him as he began anew.

I thought back to the process of helping him and realized I had more courage and hopefulness on his behalf than I was able to muster for myself. He was rebuilding his life and I was still stuck. He was going ahead and I was going nowhere. I gave him some good advice but had not considered how I might use it for myself.

I recently read Bruce Fisher and Robert Alberti's book, *Rebuilding When Your Relationship Ends.* They were realistic about the challenge lying ahead, likening it to climbing a mountain. They also saw survival and even prosperity as possible. It seemed a long way off to me.

What I would tell myself if I were sitting in a chair opposite me in my counseling room? I would first listen and try to understand the weight of feeling hopeless. I would help this other me consider what resources were available. Who could help with this challenge? Have you ever had to face anything difficult before? How did you do it? You obviously survived or you wouldn't be reading this. What did you learn from your former challenges that you could use now?

Once I started thinking this way, I began to realize that life was not overwhelming even though it seemed that way at times. I could improve my situation. Not only did I have resources of my own, help which I did not know existed found me. By being open to rebuilding, I invited people into my life. I never imagined they could mean so much to me or be so helpful.

I have reached a point in my life where I am happy to wake up and face each new day rather than dreading it. I remember Napoleon Hill's statement that each adversity has within it the seeds of an at least equal benefit. I had no idea what that meant when I first heard it. I have since learned that it means I have to be open to the gifts God leaves along my path, even if they are covered with dead leaves and need to be brushed off to be appreciated.

Life Lab Lessons

- Do you suggest actions for others you have not followed yourself?
- Why would you expect others to follow advice you would not follow?
- Do your assumptions about life hold you back like mine did?
- Use your imagination to consider how life could be different.
- Do what you have to in order to reach your dream.

Banishing Shame

One day at a time--this is enough.
Do not look back and grieve over the past for it is gone;
and do not be troubled about the future, for it has not yet come
Live in the present, and make it so beautiful
it will be worth remembering.

~Author Unknown~

Shame does not sound like a very good thing. Thoughts which usually come to mind are those of embarrassment or blushing in situations we do not like others to see us in. Yet there is a good side to shame. It is the basis of our conscience which tells us whether we are acting in a way which matches our values. Shame can be a signal that our behavior is straying from the way we would like to be seen, and a notice that we need to get back on track.

We have all heard people's behavior described as "shameless." We usually mean they are not listening to their conscience. Or more likely, they are not acting the way we think is right. Healthy shame is something we learn from supportive and nourishing parents who also set appropriate limits for us. This is how we learn a sense of responsibility as we grow. Being raised by parents with emotional balance and who accept responsibility for themselves is the best way for us to learn responsibility for ourselves.

There are extremes of responsibility. Taking too much responsibility is neurotic while not taking enough responsibility is characteristic of personality disorder like the pattern shown by criminals. The balance is an appropriate sense of responsibility for our own behavior and not an over concern for others' behavior.

John Bradshaw in *Healing the Shame That Binds You* defines toxic shame as a "pervasive sense that I am flawed and defective as a human being." With toxic shame, we do not judge our behavior as out of kilter with our beliefs, as in healthy shame, but feel there is something wrong with us as people. Our very being is worthless. It doesn't matter what we do or say. We are basically no good.

If we are stuck with the idea that we are worthless, there is no point in trying to better ourselves since we will still feel worthless. People who feel toxic shame try to hide from others. No one wants to go around with everyone laughing at them as a poor excuse for a human being. It is almost like going out in public naked and trying to hold your head up.

Babies do not show a sense of shame. They express their emotions freely, whether joy, sorrow, fear or pain, and never stop to think if it is okay to feel the way they do. Toxic shame is learned. Sometimes it is handed down for generations.

Think of parents who have been raised to see themselves as worthless. They will not be very secure about themselves and probably will continue to struggle as adults to find ways to feel good. What do such parents have to offer their children? Not much. They might look to their children to supply love and affirmation not provided by their own parents.

Their children do not know this and will act like children, sometimes loving and sometimes hating their parents. Parents raised with toxic shame will take any sign of rejection by their children personally and see it as further proof they are a failure.

They also have trouble helping their children feel good about themselves. The pattern continues for another generation.

The first step is to recognize how we feel and stop blaming ourselves and our parents for our feelings of shame. Realizing we are caught in a generational pattern of shame including our parents, grandparents, and probably other ancestors is the first step toward recovery. Knowing that we have been taught to see ourselves as shameful also tells us that it is possible to eventually feel more positive and emotionally healthy. People who see themselves as shameful tend to hide so no one else will see their shame. Overcoming toxic shame involves learning to come out of hiding. John Bradshaw talks about a variety of ways to do this.

One is to have more meaningful contact with people. Sharing our feelings and ideas with others who care about us is one way to learn that we can be accepted for who we are. Our feelings are not so different from those of others and in fact might be quite normal for what we have experienced in life.

Finding a healthy person who can give us honest feedback is a way of correcting the shame that has been instilled in us by parents who themselves lived in shame. This does not mean jumping into a romantic relationship as a way of healing ourselves. Trying to combine romance and growth out of shame may well lead to seeing our partners as substitute parents and developing unhealthy dependence on them. It is better for our recovery to wait until we feel good about ourselves before tying to form a romantic relationship. It will make for a much healthier relationship as well.

Keeping a journal about our past shaming experiences is a good way of getting distance from them and making sense of them. Writing about feelings is a good way to become more objective about them and untangle the knot of mixed feelings.

Focusing on the things we like about ourselves is a good way of starting to feel worthwhile. In shame, we tend to discount our good points and focus on our flaws. Rejoicing in our strengths and sharing our gifts with others is a good way to change the pattern. Keeping a gratitude journal each day, writing five things we are grateful for, keeps us focused on the positive.

To be human is to be imperfect. If we were perfect there would be no need to go on living. Life is a chance to work toward being the best we can be. Our best will never be perfect and that's okay. Getting to our best involves making mistakes along the way. That's okay too.

Recovery from shame means learning to handle criticism in a healthy way rather than always taking it to heart. If we are wrong, we can admit it without becoming defensive.

If we hurt people, we can let them know we realize how our behavior has hurt them. Sometimes you can confront toxic people with their characteristics which make them upset with our behavior. Sometimes the best approach is to just walk away without feeling responsible for making everyone feel happy.

Recovery from toxic shame is a complex process. We can take some of the steps just mentioned, find a support group to help us recover or seek counseling to sort things out and learn better habits. It is important to realize we have learned to feel toxic shame but we can also learn to love and appreciate ourselves as well as committing ourselves to the steps which will lead us to recovery from shame.

Life Lab Lessons

- Do you know what shame feels like?

- Do you have an underactive conscience providing little guidance?

- Do you have an overactive conscience stifling your creativity?

- Can you keep feelings of shame in perspective?

- Learn to accept yourself as a good but not perfect person.

Joseph G. Langen

Coming to Understand
Aggression and Violence

Violence is the last refuge of the incompetent.

~Salvor Hardin~

With all the aggression and violence in the world, I have been wondering what makes people become this way. It is easy to shake our heads at those in other countries, or for that matter in different neighborhoods, who become violent. We tend to write them off as "not like us." But are they so different? What if we look at ourselves? Okay, what if I look at myself?

I grew up in a family where my mother's relatives were all peace loving. My uncle who had been in the infantry during World War II never talked about his war experiences as far as I know. At my grandfather's wake, no one could recall a time when he ever became angry. My father's relatives, although they never came to blows, seemed to always be arguing about something. I take after my mother's relatives. Still there have been a couple times when my anger got best of me.

In elementary school, we had a neighborhood bully who had his way at the playground and seemed to delight in intimidating me. I put up with it for quite a while. One day in the middle of winter, he threw one too many snowballs at me. I enlisted a friend and together we threw him in a ditch and stuffed his clothes with snow. He got the message and after that was at least civil.

When I was learning to drive, my father's comments and tone of voice expressed his displeasure with my efforts to master the art of driving. He upbraided me constantly for "attempting to jar his eye teeth loose." While stopped at a store on a family outing, one last comment pushed me over the edge. I don't remember what it was but it might have had to do with his eye teeth. I turned around and for about ten minutes regaled him with every action and comment of his which had built up my resentment for years. I don't know if I accomplished anything but I did feel better for the moment.

As I grew up, I learned there were better ways of approaching such problems and never again had to resort to such extremes to get my point across. I can't say I have never since felt intimidated, powerless or wronged. But at least I have more options available to me now.

There does not seem to be agreement on what leads people to violence and aggression. A study of children suggests their degree of aggression is influenced by their seeing aggression, being the object of aggression, not having the opportunity to develop emotional bonds with others, being rewarded for aggression and being with others who engage in and encourage aggression and violent behavior.

Respect for ourselves and for others might be a key ingredient in reducing the violence in the world and in the personal lives of each of us.

Life Lab Lessons

- Think about the times you might have been violent in your life.

- If you were able to stop short of violence, how you did it?

- Consider influences in your life which encouraged you to be more aggressive.

- Consider the influences which led you to be more peaceful.

- How can you have a positive influence on someone in your life whose aggression bothers you?

Getting to Know Your Anger

Anger is never without a reason, but seldom with a good one.

~Benjamin Franklin~

What are you supposed to do with anger? Some people blast the nearest person regardless of what their anger is about, often leaving the other person confused and wondering what he or she did wrong. Some people swallow their anger, never directly expressing it, so that it eventually takes its toll on their well-being. It seems there must be a middle course between exploding and imploding.

A former Abbot at the Abbey of the Genesee, Father John Eudes Bambauer, suggests five steps to use in approaching our anger. The first is, "Allow angry feelings to come to awareness and have a careful look at them." This is a deceptively simple suggestion.

Anger is an emotion, as are joy, surprise and fear. Emotions do not arise by themselves. The psychologist Albert Ellis describes becoming emotional as a three step process. First something happens. Second we tell ourselves something about what happened. As a result of what we tell ourselves, we end up with an emotion or feeling.

Consider an example regarding anger. A man is waiting at a restaurant for a date with a woman who does not show up. He starts thinking she is probably not very responsible, lied to him about wanting to have dinner with him and is not very considerate. As he entertains these thoughts, he finds himself becoming angrier.

Father John Eudes, to my mind, is suggesting we work backward to understand our feelings, in this case, anger. We move from passion to understanding. It is hard to make much sense of our anger while we are feeling it. We need to allow our tempers to cool and our brains to engage.

Let's practice on our example from above. Rather than fanning the flames of his anger with further negative thoughts, our man might put aside his emotions and become aware of his thoughts. He might come to realize he had no evidence on which to base his thoughts about his potential date. All of his thoughts are assumptions.

Just because she did not show up, he has no way of knowing whether she is responsible or not. She may have just decided she did not feel like having dinner with him and did not bother to let him know. It is also possible that she was involved in a serious car accident on the way to dinner and might be in an emergency room. His anger is based on his imagination rather than on reality. It is possible he is right but equally possible he is wrong.

Taking a careful look at the thinking behind the anger in this case indicates that it is not based on anything he knows for sure and is premature at best. Even if he is right about his assumptions, it is not the end of the world. It may also be that our man got the time or the restaurant mixed up.

In the cold light of reason, we may find our anger overdone, inappropriate or based on false assumptions. It is also possible that our anger is justified, but that is another chapter in the story.

Another consideration suggested by the Father John Eudes, in dealing with our anger is: "Part of the problem may be generalization." Frequently our arguments and the underlying anger do not stay focused on the issue at hand. Rather than expressing our anger as it relates to a particular incident, we might become mad at the whole world, indiscriminately venting about every annoyance which comes to mind.

This is another example of being carried away with our emotions and not allowing our thinking to become involved in the process. It is like using a shotgun to try to kill a fly. We expend a great deal of energy without getting much done.

It is harmful to stifle our emotions and keep them inside. This process appears to be one of the chief contributors to stress. Yet unfocused expression of anger might make us feel better for the moment, but is unlikely to result in any lasting changes. Nothing has really been addressed and we are likely to remain stuck in a pattern of becoming upset and blowing off steam.

The alternative is to engage our brain. First, we need to clarify in our own minds what is making us angry. Once we get into a bad mood, this might not be so easy. However, we can think back to what led us to feel angry. Often there are a series of small annoyances we try to ignore, but which contribute to our overall agitation if left untended. Not dealing with the little things as they arise keeps us from building up resentments and finally overreacting to "the straw that broke the camel's back."

Once we are sure why we are angry, we can decide whether we have a good reason to be angry. Someone may have upset us by accident, or even in the process of trying to be helpful.

The third step is to consider our alternatives. Sometimes we overreact and need to talk to ourselves. We may be the problem rather than someone else.

If there is indeed something people are doing to upset us, we still have several choices. The least confrontational is to explain to them why we feel when they do certain things. Presented calmly, such an explanation might well result in others' efforts not to do what we find upsetting.

Sometimes gentle hints are not enough and we may need to make our feelings known more clearly. Some people do not respond to polite statements and may need to have clear limits established. In the case of bullies or toxic people, it helps to have reinforcements available to help make the point.

In the extreme, it might be best to avoid people who are consistently aggravating us, especially if they are doing it on purpose. They are not likely to change and constant confrontation is like beating our heads against the wall.

Life Lab Lessons

- What is your style of expressing anger?
- Do you explode with little provocation?
- Do you sit on your anger until it makes you sick?
- Can you find a middle road?
- Try explaining your position and why you are upset.

Talking About Our Anger

Anger seeks its prey,-
something to tear with sharp-edged tooth and claw,
like not to go off hungry,
leaving Love To feast on milk and honeycomb at will.

~George Eliot~

I wrote above about becoming aware of our angry feelings as suggested by Father John Eudes Bambauer. His second step in dealing with anger is, "Do not hesitate to talk about angry feelings even when related to small or insignificant issues."

In the first step, we were encouraged to think carefully about our own feelings. We considered how some people take their anger out on others and some people let it eat away at themselves. Talking about our anger is a middle course.

Talking is different from attacking. It follows from reflecting on our anger and trying to make some sense of it. Once we understand it, we are in a better position to talk sensibly about it with others. We can let go of some of the emotion and focus more on the issues involved.

I have found it interesting to observe the effect on someone who is the object of strong anger or even rage. We tend to tune into the emotion and not hear what the anger is about. If you yell at children for doing something bothersome or dangerous, they will be aware of your angry emotion. They may miss entirely what made you angry in the first place.

If we decide to talk about our anger, who do we talk with? Some of us tend to talk with anyone who will listen rather than the person who is the object of our ire. This kind of talk usually takes the form of complaining rather than discussion. It is usually geared toward gaining sympathy for our position rather than working toward an understanding of what happened.

It is probably best to talk with the person who engenders our angry feelings. As we considered before, blasting them will probably not be very productive. If you think back to the last time you were blasted, you will probably remember being defensive. You might have tried to explain yourself, whether or not you did anything wrong.

Maybe you tried to placate the other person. Or you might have been concentrating on how to escape the line of fire. In any case, these defensive maneuvers do not usually lead to any great insights or resolution of the issues. We must find a more productive way to approach them.

In addition to a discussion with the person involved, we may have trusted confidantes who can help us understand our feelings when we are having trouble figuring them out on our own. They may more easily see the situation in a rational way.

I am not suggesting we use our confidantes as sounding boards to absorb our anger, but as a source of clarification. Complaining is a way of blaming someone else for how we feel. Asking for help in dealing with our anger is a way of seeking understanding of how we became angry. We might also seek help to approach the situation in a productive way.

Deciding whether we have a reason to be angry might be difficult. This will be the next step in considering our approach to anger. Stay tuned.

Life Lab Lessons

- How do you express your anger?
- Do you show it by your actions?
- Do you share how you feel in words?
- Can you expect someone to understand why you are angry if you never explain yourself?
- If someone who upsets you understands you, will you still need to be angry?

Anger Can Have Good Reasons

Consider how much more you often suffer from your anger and grief than from those very things for which you are angry and grieved.

~Marcus Antonius~

We often think of anger as a bad thing. We try to avoid angry people if possible. We don't want to get caught up in their rage and would prefer to maintain our distance and serenity if possible. There are times when anger is appropriate. We will explore Father Bambauer's third consideration about anger.

We have considered how we jump to conclusions and talk ourselves into becoming upset over minor affronts or misunderstandings. We have also looked at the alternative choice of allowing our anger into awareness, letting it become a topic of rational thought. We can use this process to decide whether there is a good reason to be angry. Having a reason implies that we think about why we are angry rather than exploding in a burst of emotion.

What are some good reasons for being angry? Perhaps the most obvious reason is deliberate physical harm to us or to someone we care about. We can be attacked out of spite or overreaction and in response are rightly angry.

A deliberate attack on our reputation can be just as harmful. Lies about us can have a broader effect than physical violence. Long after the lie, our interactions with others can remain tainted and we can be seen as having even more faults than we actually have.

Another reason for anger is betrayal of trust. We come to depend on our spouses, relatives and friends to be there when we need them. Affairs, gossip and not following through on commitments are all ways of breaking the trust on which we base our relationships. These deliberate transgressions are all legitimate reasons for us to be angry.

You may have noticed that I used the word "deliberate" in describing each of the above examples. Our anger is justified when someone makes the choice to act in a way which is harmful to us. Mistakes and misunderstandings don't count. The key element is the intention to cause us harm.

The tricky part is to know what is in someone else's mind and what his or her intentions are. Do you recall a time when your intentions were misunderstood? In the course of ordinary events it is easy enough for us to misunderstand each other's intentions. The heat of anger only complicates the task.

There are ways to judge whether an affront is deliberate and therefore worthy of our anger. We can ask others what their intentions are. Sometimes they will be honest and tell us what they had in mind. If we have told them how we feel about a certain behavior toward us, and they repeat it, there is a good chance it is on purpose.

Life Lab Lessons

- Did you ever think of anger as something positive?
- Seeing someone hurting another is an example of justifiable anger.
- Be sure you understand others' motivations when you are angry.
- Be sure you understand your own motivations.
- Try talking about it.

Our Anger Says More about Us than About Others

The ones who cannot restrain their anger will wish undone what their temper and irritation prompted them to do.

~Horace~

We have looked at a number of statements about anger by the Abbot and monk, John Eudes Bambauer. His final observation is, "Anger often reveals how you feel and think about yourself." We have considered where anger comes from, whether it is justified and some options we have for dealing with it. Up to now we have thought about anger as being a response to something that happens to us.

Father John Eudes suggests in his last statement on the subject that we may learn more about ourselves from considering our anger than about the objects of our anger. Some people are chronically angry. No matter what the situation, they seem to find something annoying about it deserving of their anger. We may recall times when we were in a bad mood, tired or frustrated, and it took very little to annoy us.

Becoming angry gives us a chance to understand ourselves a little better. What is there about us that inclines us to become angry? After all, we could also see the humor in difficult situations or take them in stride. We could reach conclusions which on reflection appear bizarre. We don't deserve to be treated the way we are. God is being unfair by piling so much trouble on us at once. People should know better than to annoy us when we have a great deal on our minds.

We could stop to examine our thoughts as we are invited to do by Father John Eudes. Have you ever told yourself one of things in the above paragraph? Are any of them true? Is it up to us to decide how we deserve to be treated? Do we have the right to decide what is fair for God to do? Who are we to decide what others should know?

When we get angry, we might not just be reacting to the present situation. We may have leftover feelings from childhood inclining us to expect to be treated poorly. Maybe we jump to the same conclusion in the present. Were we spoiled earlier in life and now expect everyone to anticipate and kowtow to our wants and needs? Do we have high standards for ourselves and expect others to live up to our code of conduct, becoming angry when they don't.

All of these considerations of anger were made by a contemplative monk who has had many hours to think about the meaning of his life, God's will for us and the implications of our response to His will. Most of us do not have regular times for contemplation built into our daily schedule. However there is no reason we can't put aside time to consider the meaning of our lives. Doing so may help put our lives and our experiences into context so we can see the larger picture. From this perspective, our anger loses its bite and our feelings become less important in the larger context of creation.

If you are interested in more of the thoughts of Father Bambauer, they are discussed in some detail by Henri J. Nouwen in his book, *The Genesee Diary.*

Life Lab Lessons

- If you feel angry, who do you blame for it?

- Do you take responsibility for your feeling?

- Do you blame someone else?

- Think about what leads to your anger.

- What can you do to reduce your anger regardless of others' actions?

Chapter 6

Finding Our Creativity

We tend to think of creativity as reserved for artists and performers. We all have a creative side. Unfortunately it can be extinguished by the time we reach second grade in attempts to socialize us. You might have to listen and watch closely as your creative side emerges sheepishly from the shadows.

*****

Understanding Art and the Artist Within

You know that a blank wall is an appalling thing to look at: the wall of a museum - a canvas - a piece of film - or a guy sitting in front of a typewriter. Then, you start out to do something - that vague thing called creation. The beginning strikes awe within you.

~Edward Steichen~

I once knew a painter who had difficulty with periodic depression. He painted only during his episodes of depression and was able to put on paper the feelings which troubled him. His paintings were dark, murky and presented visible evidence of his depression. Yet it also meant that the depression was outside him rather than locked within him.

I also knew a sculptor who had similar difficulty with depression. In contrast to the first artist, he created his sculptures only during the periods when he was not experiencing depression. He wanted to keep his art separate from his depression and did not want it to contaminate his creative process.

Since I met these two artists many years ago, I have often wondered about the relationship between the inner life of the artist and what he or she produces. It was interesting to me that the first artist mainly painted people. The second produced only abstract pieces. One artist was interested in relationships and the other in structure.

I am not an expert on art and am not an accomplished artist although I dabble in watercolor, acrylic and poster paints. I am still very much an amateur artist. I struggle with the basics of representing what I see. I have not yet mastered the mechanics enough to concentrate on what I want to communicate. I remember years ago being troubled about where my life was heading. I remember singing with passion and desperation.

Feelings are often difficult to put into words. Our pain can keep us from even saying the words. We might wonder whether our words will be understood. Sometimes we do not even understand our own feelings.

Art can express the wordless emotions we feel or allow us to put or feelings on exhibit for others to consider. People approach art in their own way and make of it what they will through the veil of their own perceptions. This process happens with words as well, but sometimes we express ourselves more subtly through art. We do not feel quite as exposed. Sometimes artists hide meanings in their work available only to others who understand those feelings.

People do not always create art for others to see. They might start with the idea of a publicly viewed work and then change their minds. I remember some time ago sitting with my friend John who had written a biography of Andy Warhol. As we sat together, he fed the pages of his book into the fire. I begged him to allow me to read it first, but he could not agree to this for his own reasons which remained hidden from me. Whatever art means to the artist or to its viewers, it is a powerful way to express what otherwise might remain unstated.

Life Lab Lessons

- Visit a Mental Health Association art exhibit, the Mental Health Coalition's Impressions Gallery in Rochester or another exhibit of works by those dealing with mental illness.

- See if you can find messages within those paintings which represent your own feelings.

- Visit an art gallery and look for the artists' feelings.

- Talk with an artist about his or her art.

- Try your hand at art and see what feelings of yours emerge.

Choose to Dance

On with dance, let joy be unconfined, is my motto;
whether there's any dance to dance or any joy to unconfine.

~Mark Twain~

In a recent visit, my friend Judy shared with me Mark Sanders' and Tia Sillers' book *I Hope You Dance*. How often do we dance, literally or figuratively? Many of us trudge through life, plodding along as if there were no joy around us. The news is full of conflict, disagreement and portents of worse things to come.

During a recent summer, I attended a professional dance performance and quite a few neighborhood concerts. Most of them led to toe tapping or outright dancing. The elderly seemed to prefer the waltz, the middle aged showed off their swing dance and children flew around the floor with abandon, sometimes in tune with the music and sometimes with their own inner rhythms. Some dancers had their own styles. Among them were "the walker, the hopper and the smokers."

Although limited in my own dance repertory, my toes were frequently tapping and I did get up for the occasional swing dance. I have been fascinated by dance since my friend John got me back stage to watch the Rockettes at Radio City Music Hall many years ago. People breaking into a spontaneous dance shake me out of my inner world and gladdens my heart. I am not sure why. It just happens.

Most cultures have their own dances to express joy, fear, hopes or sorrow. Often our bodies can release emotions when words fail us. Dance transcends language. We can misinterpret what others say to us, but it is harder to misunderstand someone else's dance. Our dances always seem to enrich each other's lives while our words can sometimes make everyone feel worse.

Maybe we are too attached to the meaning of our words and expect others to understand them. They might hear something different from what we intend. Maybe we have fewer expectations of our dance and don't worry so much about how others will receive it. Maybe we are just dancing and don't even have a message hidden in our steps.

I remember an exercise I experienced last summer at a conference on creativity. We each spent some time painting whatever we wanted. When we were finished painting we broke up into pairs. The painter danced an interpretation of what he or she had just painted. Then the observer danced a response to the painting. I can't put into words what it meant, since the meaning was on another level where words don't reach. But we each felt a connection to the painting and to each other beyond what our words could allow.

I just had a strange thought while I was writing this. What if we danced for each other when we first met rather than trying to communicate with words? What if representatives of countries danced for each other at the United Nations rather than haggling about their own national interests? It would certainly make for a different world.

Life Lab Lessons

- Sometime when you are alone, dance for yourself.

- Think about what your dance says to you.

- Dance for someone you care about without using any words.

- Ask the other person to dance for you.
- Think about how your dance and your words differ.

Finding Creativity in Winter

The creative is the place where no one else has ever been. You have to leave the city of your comfort and go into the wilderness of your intuition. What you'll discover will be wonderful. What you'll discover is yourself.

~Alan Alda~

I usually think of winter as a time when nature lies dormant. The color disappears from many plants and trees and some plants disappear underground not to be seen again until spring. I sometimes look at the drifting snow and think of the world hibernating.

I have done much of my drawing and painting in the summer, sitting on my front porch. Both books I have written were largely composed on my porch in summer. In the past I have thought of my creativity as burying itself in the mud at the bottom of a pond like a turtle.

This past year has been different for some reason. In early winter I found it difficult to write and had to force myself to sit at the computer or get my pen moving on a pad. My easel stood empty and my paints remained capped in their tubes.

Then last week I picked up a pencil and started drawing on the empty paper lying at the ready on my easel. Next I got out some paints and started drawing abstract designs and human figures. Then I noticed that, after painting, words came to me much more easily when I sat down to write. I don't know how this happened.

I remember one summer many years ago when I had a chance to spend a week at a friend's cabin on Duck Lake in Interlaken, Michigan. I had been working quite hard and had no time to write for a while. I relished the chance to have some time to sit on the shore and write stories. The first morning after I arrived, I found a convenient rock, got comfortable by the lake with the sun rising and loons lazily swimming by. I opened my notebook, took the cap off my pen and sat there ready to write. Nothing came out of the pen. Nothing stirred in my head.

I knew that I had neglected my muse and that she would not reappear until she was darn good and ready. I managed a few pages that week. I realized that I don't have control over my creativity but can only be ready for it to appear. I can't force ideas into my head and can't make words come out of my pen or images come from my pencil or brush. It is my job to listen and watch for ideas to appear and be ready to capture them when they do.

Both that summer and this winter have humbled me and made me thankful for all the words and images which have arisen in my mind over the years. I came to realize that I do not possess creative ideas. They possess me and invite me to share them with others.

Life Lab Lessons

- Think about ways you have been creative in your life.
- What creative ideas have popped into your mind lately?
- What did you do about them?
- Be open to your own creativity today.
- Don't be afraid to share what you find with others.

Learn to Appreciate Music as a Common Language

Music washes away from the soul the dust of everyday life.

~Berthold Auerbach~

Recently I heard the Buffalo Symphony Orchestra perform in Centennial Park in Batavia. This was the latest in a series of concerts I have had the pleasure of attending. I got to thinking about the place of music in our lives. Eventually I began to consider the contribution of music to civilization throughout history and across civilizations.

In college I attended Kabuki and Noh theater performances and also saw Chinese Opera. I found the music foreign to my ear and difficult to comprehend although I saw others in the audience who appeared quite comfortable with it.

Opera, symphony, folk and rap aficionados inhabit worlds which seldom intersect. Yet they all find rapture in their own forms of music. It may be difficult for devotees to find anything in common with other forms of music. Some music speaks to us in words while others rely on melody and rhythm.

What does music mean to us? Since lyrics can be secondary to music or lacking altogether, it can be hard to find words to express what music means to us. We might be left with only the emotions which music suggests and portrays.

Most of us can appreciate musical expression of joy, happiness and anticipation even if the music's form is foreign to us. More difficult is learning to appreciate expression of pain, anger and hurt in unfamiliar music. Music often expresses emotions shared by the people of the culture in which it develops. We use music to celebrate, express our desires and grieve. We listen to lullabies when we are born. Dirges punctuate our funerals.

Archeological findings tell us that music was present in the earliest civilizations in one form or another, beginning with primitive drums. Throughout the centuries musical instruments have taken on increasingly complex forms. Have you ever considered the workings of a pipe organ? Despite the complexity of instruments, a recent concert at the Eastman Theater during the Rochester International Jazz Festival featured instruments constructed and played by musicians from Mali.

It's easy for us to misinterpret the meaning of each others' words, even when we have a common language. We assume that we know what others are saying, jump to conclusions about our differences from them and even see ourselves as superior to them. Words sometimes trip us and make it difficult for us to understand each other. What if we look at each other from another perspective and if we try to understand the place of music in each others' lives, attempting to see and hear the feelings music expresses? Maybe such an approach would help us appreciate each other a little better without becoming lost in words.

Life Lab Lessons

- Listen to the music you like and consider why you like it.
- What emotions or life outlook does your music express?
- Are you comfortable with the emotions or life outlook?
- Listen to others' music and see if you can tell what it means to them.
- If you can't, try asking them.

What Moving Has Taught Me

Without change, something sleeps inside us, and seldom awakens.
The sleeper must awaken.

~Frank Herbert~

For several weeks, I was busy sorting through the remains of my life so far in preparation for a move from Batavia to Leroy. During the process I discovered long forgotten memories.

I found books from my graduate studies in psychology including works of psychologists from the 1880's. My favorite novels surfaced, including those of John Updike, Mark Twain, and John Irving. Art, history and gardening books reappeared as did musical scores.

I came across files I had been saving for some unexpected need. Maybe I could use the information for a particularly difficult client. Perhaps I would want to write a column and find relevant information at hand without having to search for it.

My plants wanted to know if they were invited to move to Leroy. They were. My bicycle was also anxious to try out some new routes. It will get the chance. My racquetball racquet looked imploringly at me. Afraid not, I don't think I'm up to it any more. Various pieces of furniture also vied to be included. My desks, file cabinets as well as art work and bookshelves my son made for me over the years made the cut. My waterbed, several chairs and appliances didn't.

But all that's just stuff. What do I take of myself? My memories of course. My stuff brings back my memories, but I will have to forgo the visible reminders in some cases and rely on my mind alone. Over the years others have reminded me of events in my life which I am hard pressed to recall. I don't need to remember everything. Besides I can't carry around a houseful of stuff just for their attached memories. Or at least I choose not to.

I also take with me what I have learned about life over the years. I don't think I could sit down and write a list of my life learnings. But they do come back to me when I need them and I remember my past mistakes and what I learned from them.

I take my relationships with me. Some of the people I have met are long dead. Some are lost to me and I don't know what has become of them. Some were lost but found again to my great joy. Some have always been with me and still are. The people who have passed through my life have provided me with my greatest joy. Some have presented trials, but hopefully I have learned from them all.

I don't know what awaits me in the next incarnation of my life. I no longer fear what might happen and look forward to the new adventures which await me. I hope to be creative in my response to them.

Life Lab Lessons

- What are your fondest memories?
- What are you glad to leave behind you?
- What do you look forward to?
- Do you enjoy the challenge of each day's adventures?
- Are there any course corrections you wish to consider?

Reconnecting with My Muse

*Each of the arts whose office is to refine, purify, adorn,
embellish and grace life is under the patronage of a muse,
no god being found worthy to preside over them.*

~Ralph Waldo Emerson~

There is no classical Greek muse for fiction, yet I have a fiction muse. There was none for roller skating either, yet one appeared in the movie Xanadu. Something in that movie excited me. Was it Olivia Newton-John or her character? I thought it might be a rekindling of my adolescent fantasies. Partly by fate and partially by choice, I have not yet finished being an adolescent. After seeing the movie three times, I realized that there was something more here for me than just a movie. It took a while to figure out what stirred me.

For years, there has been an extra feminine presence around my house. It was not my wife or either of my two daughters. It was more than the female presence of the dog or cat. At first, it was very ethereal, like the memory of a purple dressing gown from Victoria's Secret. There was no form, at least none that was well defined.

She does have other sensory qualities. I can hear her swish by or rustle near me. I can feel her warmth and softness against my shoulder or thigh. At times, I have been aware of a faint lavender scent. I can feel her closeness and the weight of ideas she offers me. I am aware of her restlessness when I choose to read rather than write and her disappointment when I watch television.

She first appeared after I attended a noontime concert, inspiring me to write a story about music and schizophrenia. I had not planned to write the story. I had written nothing creative since my bungling attempts in high school English class. All I had published were newspaper articles about mental health. All I had written recently were psychological test reports.

I had a new computer. I knew enough about computers to know that there were no ideas inside. All the computer could do was say yes or no, although it did so in some very sophisticated ways. I sat at the computer and somehow my fingers typed the first story. Other stories followed, without my realizing where they originated or why I felt compelled to write them.

I found out the hard way that muses do not like being ignored. I decided that I needed to concentrate on my finances for a while rather than on my writing. Shortly after that I found my attempts to write yielded wooden outlines, stony starts and ideas which scattered like feathers in the wind.

Nothing worked. She was gone. Reading fiction prompted new ideas. Writer's Digest provided tools. Writer's Market listed publishing prospects. All too late. Nothing worked.

I thought she was gone for good. I guess I deserved it. I never thought much about how to entertain a muse. I have since come to realize that muses are much like people. If there is nothing to interest them, they move on. I did not invite her to come to me in the first place, and did not know how to get her back. Maybe somebody else could use the books I had bought about writing. I could go back to enjoying others' fiction.

While driving to northern Michigan, I tired of thinking about money. My thoughts drifted to floating in the lake, hearing the squawk of the imported peacock and being transformed by the classic but youthful music at Interlochen National Music Camp.

Sitting at the picnic table outside the cabin on the second day, I realized my muse was back. The swish was there, the warmth. Was that lavender in the air? I had another chance. But which muse was she? She was not Polyphonia. My work could scarcely be called sacred poetry. She did not appear to be Erato, Euterpe or Calliope. I don't write love poetry, lyric poetry or epic poetry. What I do can not be considered astronomy, so she could not be Urania. My work is read, not staged. Therefore, it could not be inspired by Terpsichore, famed for choral song and dance. I clearly write fiction and not history, eliminating Clio. My writing does not feel like tragedy or comedy, leaving out Melpomene and Thalia.

That was nine. There were no muses left. Then I recalled that muses are not fond of revealing themselves fully. Nor, as I should have been aware, are they particularly logical. Yet there I was trying to figure her out. One of them must be my muse. Since there is none for fiction, she must be Calliope, the muse of epic poetry and the one most likely to take an interest in my writing.

Learning from past mistakes, I finally realized that my job was to make her comfortable, give her space in my mind, and listen to what she whispered to me. I will have to take better care of her. Next time she leaves, she might not come back.

Life Lab Lessons

- Where does your creativity originate?
- Do you take credit for it?
- Do you depend on outside inspiration?
- How do you find your creative stimulus?
- Give your Muse the respect she deserves.

Chapter 7

Stress and Life

We hear more about stress these days than we ever did before. It takes the blame for murder sprees, illness and feeling paralyzed in our daily lives. Yet stress can motivate us to get moving when we might otherwise be complacent. Surprisingly, good fortune can also be stressful. Take a deep breath and get going.

*****

Stressful Situations Come in Many Different Degrees

Stress is basically a disconnection from the earth, a forgetting of the breath. Stress is an ignorant state. It believes that everything is an emergency. Nothing is that important. Just lie down.

~Natalie Goldberg~

There are many degrees of stress from mild annoyance to feeling overwhelmed. If everything is going well, we take fairly large amounts of stress in stride. Under more trying circumstances an otherwise minor stress may put us over the top. If the stressful situation in question is the only one we face all week, it is not so bad. If we have ten of them to deal with at once, it is a different story.

Sometimes we have little control over the amount of stress we have to face at any given time. Sometimes we contribute to our stress. For example, high mortgages, car payments and credit card bills come from our choice of lifestyle. We could have chosen to live in a way which did not involve these stresses.

We do not often stop to ponder our stress. Whether we are aware of it or not, our thinking has a considerable effect on how we react to a stressful situation.

Consider an example. Suppose you are walking down the street and someone bumps into you. Do you get upset? If you see this person bumping into everyone in front of you on purpose and laughing, you would probably get quite angry. If the person is distracted by a conversation, and is not watching where he is going, you might get less angry. If the person is carrying a white cane and obviously can't see you, how angry would you get? You would probably have three different reactions depending on how you see the circumstances and what you tell yourself about them.

Even if we think we are reacting to someone else's behavior, we are actually reacting to what we tell ourselves about their behavior rather than to how they act. We can become angry if we feel slighted by someone regardless of whether they know we feel slighted. We choose to avoid some of our stress by taking others' actions less personally.

How have we come to feel so much stress these days? I think part of the answer lies in cultural changes. Two hundred years ago, people struggled for survival and had little time to consider what their lives were like. Focus was on survival. I am not sure life was any less stressful then, but people took pressure for granted.

We don't expect the burden of stress and are surprised when it hits us between the eyes. We forget that stressful situations are a part of life, that we have some control over these situations and that we have choices about how to react to them. Next time you are feeling under stress, think about how you got there. Concentrate less on how awful it is and more on what you can do about it.

Life Lab Lessons

- Do you realize not all stress is the same?

- Do you react to inconveniences the same way you react to disasters?

- Do you always know the difference?

- If you have control of the situation, take effective action to change it.

- If you can't control it, minimize its effect and move on.

Dealing with Stress and Its Discontents

The only pressure I'm under is the pressure I've put on myself.

~Mark Messier~

I find it hard lately to drive anywhere without finding another car ten feet behind me, desperately seeking a way to pass me. Television commercials shout at prospective buyers or bombard them with frenetic claims overlapping one another. Newspaper and magazine articles blame stress for physical and emotional ailments. Lately, I have noticed more reports of murder and suicide in cases where people apparently find life intolerable.

Sigmund Freud wrote a book called *Civilization and Its Discontents*. Without belaboring Freud's comments, two statements from the introduction struck me. One is his observation that people would rather suffer than change. The other is a summary of the book's theme that as long as there is culture, people will be unhappy.

I didn't like reading either statement. I prefer to think that people can change in a way which makes their lives more satisfying or at least more tolerable. I also don't like the idea that culture makes people unhappy. Would we be any happier in an uncivilized world?

Certainly civilization means that our world is more complex. Our lives in a civilized society consist of more than hunting, eating, procreating and dying. I think it would be fair to say that founders of the world's great civilizations sought to make the world a better place in which to live at least for their own citizens.

So where did stress come from? At one time people were so focused on survival that they had no extra time or energy to consider how they felt about their lives. Vacations, weekends and time for relaxation just didn't exist. Now they do. We have come to rely on our leisure and even expect it as our birthright. Maybe unexpected inconvenience leads to stress. We tell ourselves we have a right to life on our own terms. We have forgotten that life is a combination of joy, learning and discovery accompanied by sorrow, loss and grief.

How can we deal with stress? First we should consider how much stress we create through our expectations. If we are convinced that life should involve no disappointments or inconvenience, we are bound to feel off kilter. Our frantic efforts to tailor the world to our convenience can't lead to anything but stress. We can avoid much of our stress by accepting the world as we find it rather than trying to force it into the mold we would like.

I remember Eckhard Tolle saying that we have three choices when faced with a situation we don't like. We can accept the situation as it is. We can do what is possible to change the situation and then move on. We can also become upset about it. What's your choice?

Life Lab Lessons

- How do you deal with uncomfortable situations?
- Are you satisfied with your approach?
- How else can you react?
- Ask yourself whether your expectations of life are realistic.
- If not, how can you adjust your expectations?

Stop Making Problems of Life Situations

Whether you're winning or losing, it is important to always be yourself. You can't change because of the circumstances around you.

~Cotton Fitzsimmons~

Oprah has been featuring Eckhart Tolle lately in a series of interviews about his book, The New Earth. I decided to review my copy of his earlier book, *The Power of Now*, which lays the groundwork for *The New Earth*. His words interested me since I have spent so many years listening to people's problems in my work as a psychologist.

He described a problem as "dwelling on a situation mentally without there being a true intention or possibility of taking action now and making it part of your sense of self." I wish I had thought of problems that way when I was counseling. This reflection keeps popping into my mind every time I hear people complaining about situations in their lives.

Tolle went on to say that there are situations in all of our lives which we would prefer were not present. Sometimes we can do something about them. Rather than dwelling on how bad the situation is, this is the time to do something about it. Get on with it and don't get stuck making it a problem.

Sometimes there is not much we can do about a situation, at least for now. In that case, the best we can do is accept the situation as it is and move on. Perhaps there will be something we can do about it in the future.

But what happens if we don't take either approach? I can think of a time when I made my financial insecurity a problem. For quite a while, I did nothing about it. I just worried about it. I worried that I would never be able to retire, that I would be stuck paying off bills for the rest of my life and that I would not have the money to do the things which were important to me.

I could find no acceptable answer on my own. Finally, I got tired of worrying and asked people I thought could help me what I might do about it. Eventually, I learned how to stop worrying and do what I could to change my situation. How I did this is another story which I will tell some other time.

In the quote above, Tolle tells us what will happen if we continue to dwell on the situation and make it a problem. It becomes part of our sense of self. We make it our own and even start defining ourselves as a person with that particular problem. We are stuck regretting our past and worrying about our future. What a waste of our time. All we have is right now. We have the more viable choices of doing something about our situation or accepting it.

Life Lab Lessons

- Do you have situations in your life you think of as problems?

- How much time to you spend worrying about them?

- What can you do right now about a problem situation?

- If you can't do anything, how about accepting it for the time being?

- If you insist on worrying, how about setting aside part of each day for worrying?

How to Find the Seeds of an Equal Benefit

It is how people respond to stress that determines
whether they will profit from misfortune or be miserable.

~Mihaly Csikszentmihalyi~

I was thinking recently about Napoleon Hill's statement that inside every adversity lie the seeds of an at least equal benefit. Good results can follow bad experiences. I have had times in my life when things looked quite bleak. Each time I learned something useful from the experience.

My wise friend, Steve D'Annunzio, has frequently reminded me that adversity, particularly in the form of illness, is God's way of telling us there is something in our lives that needs attention. Judging by the magnitude of adversity piled on some of us, Big Ben must sometimes be necessary when we don't pay attention to the snooze alarm.

Three people of my acquaintance have recently been diagnosed with cancer, one in the late stages. A good friend of mine is mired in serious depression. I wondered what the message is for them. As I thought about it, I realized I don't have to understand their message. It is theirs, not mine. My job is to heed my own messages.

We are often too busy with troublesome emotions to hear the message. We may be angry at God for torturing us. Some of us, troubled by human suffering, have concluded that there could not be a loving God who would inflict such torture on His creatures.

Others of us become preoccupied with feeling sorry for ourselves. We look around and do not see others with the same problems as ours. Why should we have to put up with such troubles? It isn't fair!

Still others of us are overcome by fear. What will become of us? How will we manage life with the burdens we have to bear? Will we ever be able to get back to our old selves?

If being angry, sad or fearful doesn't help, what are we to do? The first step is to back off from our immediate emotional responses. We need to learn to be still within ourselves. Maybe that is part of the message. I heard somewhere that when God speaks to us, He/She does not shout but whispers. If there is too much noise in our minds, we can't hear the message. Meditation, time in the woods or a prayerful attitude can all open our minds.

Once we are in a receptive state, what do we do with the message? Remember the seeds we started out with? Seeds are not very impressive in themselves. Given care, nurturing, and time, they can become giant redwood trees. People also start as seeds.

What wonders might be hiding in the seeds of the benefits awaiting us? Let's consider an example. Someone I know ended up filing for bankruptcy. He entertained feelings of fear, sadness and depression. He was invited by people who cared about him to look at how he could start living his life with a sense of prosperity. Now he is doing better financially than he ever dreamed. He is not wealthy but has learned to respect money and himself.

Life Lab Lessons:

- How can I put aside my troubled feelings?

- How can I still my mind and heart?

- What do I hear when I start to listen?

- What new aspects of my life await me?

- Can I let go of control and let God be God?

How to Rise to the Challenge of Good Fortune

It takes more strength of character to withstand good fortune than bad.

~François de La Rochefoucauld~

Do you know that good fortune can be stressful? Some religious groups in the past have seen good fortune as a message from God. They took the message to mean those receiving the benefits were favored by God more than the less fortunate. It was an opportunity for gloating and self satisfaction. That message suggests that we don't have to do anything else and have already made it into God's grace.

I have always felt that if there were nothing left to accomplish, there would be no need to go on living. We tend to take good fortune for granted. I would guess that, for most of us, our thoughts and prayers are directed toward what we want or don't want in our lives more than toward what we already have.

There is a bible story about ten lepers whom Jesus cured. Only one came back to thank him. The others were so busy enjoying their cure that they took it for granted.

Our good fortune could consist of greater wealth, a newfound love or even good health. Good fortune sometimes stays with us for a long time and sometimes appears suddenly, departs just as quickly. We are more likely to take ongoing blessings for granted and show greater appreciation for those which appear more dramatically.

We can think of good fortune as providing energy, whether it is physical, emotional, spiritual or monetary. We can also look at it as an opportunity which might not be available to others. It may also be available to us for only a limited time. I have often heard people talk of waiting for retirement to follow their dreams. They might not live until retirement or might not have the same resources available if they do live that long.

There is a saying that today is the first day of the rest of your life. It might also be the last day. In any case, it is the only day we have right now. How can we put it to best use?

We might not have the same opportunity tomorrow. I remember a time when I was writing short stories with ease. I decided to take a break and wait until an upcoming vacation when I would have more time to write. When the time came, I was out of ideas.

Each new day has its own gifts, opportunities and challenges. Henry David Thoreau wrote about how he started each day at Walden Pond. Before he got out of bed, he made a list of those things for which he was grateful before going about his business for that day.

Life Lab Lessons

- What about my life today makes me feel grateful?

- What opportunities do I have today?

- If I don't take advantage of today's opportunities, how do I know I will have the same chance in the future?

- How can I share my good fortune with others?

- What challenges can I meet with the resources I have available today?

Chapter 8

People I'd Like You to Meet

I have met many people who have inspired me to change my view of life. I would like you to meet a few of them and hear their stories. How many people have you met who have helped you think differently about life? Cherish them.

*****

Haley's AD/HD

Reeling and writhing, of course, to begin with, the Mock Turtle replied, and then the different branches of arithmetic, ambition, distraction, uglification, and derision.

~Lewis Carroll, Alice's Adventures in Wonderland~

Most of what is written about AD/HD is from the point of view of professionals, teachers, or parents. Little is written from the child's perspective. Many children are befuddled by AD/HD, or embarrassed to talk about it.

Haley is an articulate ten year old girl who was diagnosed with AD/HD in first grade. Her father is in treatment for cancer. Her parents are divorced. She lives with her father and half brother. She has visitation with her mother who is remarried and has a new baby.

Haley realized there was something different about her in kindergarten or first grade. She knew something was wrong but did not know what. She later learned it was called AD/HD. She sees her parents as both having AD/HD as well as her grandparents and thinks it can be genetic for some people. Parents probably give it to their kids.

Haley has been on medication since her AD/HD was discovered. "First I was on Ritalin. Then I tried Concerta but it didn't help. Now I am back on Ritalin twice a day." She does not think her condition will ever go away and does not really care if it does since she is not bothered by it and has learned to live with it.

She finds that sometimes AD/HD helps her. "I started doodling in class and found out I wanted to be an artist. AD/HD gives me a sense of creativity." She took time out from the interview to show me some of the drawings she had finished or was working on. Despite having come to terms with her condition, she is sometimes angry about it. "It makes me mad at people and makes me blame them. I don't know how this happens."

On occasion she gets hyper during lunch. "Sometimes I act really goofy. Last week I was squawking like a chicken." Her friends have asked her why she is so hyper. She finally decided to tell them why. She explained what she knew about AD/HD to her friends and felt they understood her.

Haley finds that she has some trouble keeping friends. "I have mood swings and then get in fights with my friends." She also sometimes gets mouthy with her friends. They yell at her when she does this. Three girls on the bus still tease her about being weird, hyperactive and crazy. "A lot of kids in school make fun of me for playing with things in class."

She thinks her AD/HD makes school boring for her. "As far as subjects, math, gym and health are okay. Science and social studies are good, especially when we do hands on activities. Sometimes school is boring though." She likes micro-school where everyone has a job during the last half hour of the school day. "There is a post office, bank, restaurant and court. I work in micro media production as an artist and make signs for people."

She also has trouble doing her homework. "I lie and say I don't have any homework so I can spend more time with my father. I usually don't do homework because it's boring. When I don't do my homework, I get in trouble and am grounded or have to stay after school."

Haley does not feel she gets enough time to spend with her father. She would also like to have more time with her mother who has a new baby. She had not thought of talking with her father about having more time together, but decides to try it.

"Sometimes I tell my father or mother I hate them or don't like them any more. I don't really mean it but sometimes I just blurt it out." She would also like to see her grandparents more than she does. She takes a second pill when she goes to visit them. She thinks they spoil her. She does not think AD/HD makes any difference to them and does not think her visits with them would be any different if she did not have it.

Haley does not talk much with other kids who have AD/HD. She knows there are others in her school but does not know who they are. She was in a group for kids whose parents were divorced and remembers there being a couple kids with AD/HD in the group. "I would like to be in a group where everybody had AD/HD because they would understand what it is like for me."

She finds it easier to concentrate if what she is doing is fun or if she can work with her hands. She finds it hard to concentrate when her AD/HD is bothering her, when she thinks about her father being sick, or when TV is on.

Haley's is one voice of children with AD/HD. Her circumstances are unique to her and her perspective cannot be generalized to all children with AD/HD. Nevertheless, her story is a reminder that all children have their own understanding of their condition and reactions to it. Knowing your child's perspective on AD/HD and his or her concerns can be helpful in knowing how to be supportive.

Life Lab Lessons

- Are you always able to stay focused?

- What if you could hardly ever stay on task?

- What if you handle every situation with a "Ready, Fire, Aim
mentality?

- Don't assume everyone has the same coping skills.

- Try to understand others from how life looks to them.

Celebrating a Life- Happy Birthday Russ

Although it is generally known,
I think it's about time to announce
that I was born at a very early age.

~Groucho Marx~

Russ Van Valkenburg was born in 1928. So were Edward Albee, Maya Angelou and Alvin Toffler. Some names are known in a small community, some nationally and some worldwide. No one is born with the intention of becoming world famous.

Babies are born every minute to the delight of their families. Each baby fascinates those of us who have lived for a while and reminds us of what it means to be human. Babies discover the world about them one marvel at a time and we have the opportunity to watch their adventures.

It's easy to take life for granted until' the delight of a baby or the misfortune of an illness makes us realize just how precious life is. As the years pass, we learn to appreciate our gifts such as physical strength, intelligence, creativity and social skills. We also discover our hopes and dreams. Eventually we become aware of our limitations.

Recently I had the opportunity to participate in Russ's eightieth birthday gathering. I didn't have to do it by myself. His wife of sixty one years headed the group of well-wishers including family and friends of all ages. I counted myself fortunate to participate in his celebration. Having weathered the ups and downs which all of us encounter over the years, Russ played the gracious host, enjoying the presence of each guest and being sure everyone knew how happy he was to share his birthday with them.

Joy filled the day. I heard no harsh words, saw no cross glances and felt no antagonism from anyone in attendance. What would it be like to live in a world where everyone acted the way guests did at Russ's birthday party? What if we could all get along, find a reason to celebrate with each other and enjoy each other's company?

We tend to see ourselves as owner of our little corner of the earth rather than guests at life's party. Maybe it's all in our perspective. We don't have as much control over our lives as we would like to think. Life invites us to share in the pageant of the universe and navigate with a body we use during our time on earth. We don't know how long we will be here or what we will be able to accomplish.

We do have some control over what effect we have on people, how they think of us and how they will remember us. The house we live in, what car we drive, and how much money we accumulate aren't that important in the long run. I consider myself fortunate to be touched by the magic of Russ's life and to have had some small part in his life adventure so far.

Life Lab Lessons

- If today is your birthday, stop to count your life blessings and thank God for them.

- If it's not your birthday, count your blessings and give thanks anyway.

- Be thankful for the many people who have touched your life.

- Give thanks for those who have touched your life in silent ways.

- Celebrate the life you have to live just for today.

The Priestly Gift of Kindness

In everyone's life, at some time, our inner fire goes out. It is then burst into flame by an encounter with another human being. We should all be thankful for those people who rekindle the inner spirit.

~Albert Schweitzer~

Catholic priests have made headlines over the past few years in none too flattering a manner. It seems the only priests who appear in the news are those caught in shameful acts. We don't hear much about the high percentage of priests who do not fall into this category. For the most part, their lives are not dramatic and do not command headlines. We know little about them.

I recently attended the fiftieth anniversary jubilee celebration of my uncle's priesthood. Although I had an idea what kind of person he is, many of the details of his life remained quietly unnoticed, at least to me.

I always knew him as a man of peace. Yet he fought for our country in the Battle of the Bulge in World War II. He seldom discussed his war experiences and, when he did, never talked about the terror and desperation of war.

When he returned from military service, he brought with him a toy Scottie dog which remained my constant companion for years and always reminded me of him. His disposition was very much like my grandfather's. Father Richard has been compassionate, generous and humble, qualities noted by those who came to know him during the course of his priesthood. He never sought or found fame, wealth or power. One speaker said he gave much to others and took little. Unless you know him personally, it would be easy to pass him by without notice.

Priests view their vocations as a call to service from God rather than a choice they make. In his case, it was not as dramatic as being knocked off a horse as the bible story describes happening to St. Paul. Richard described his call as a whisper from God, an almost imperceptible voice which he was not even sure was meant for him.

As he told his story, I thought of Francis Thompson's poem, The Hound of Heaven, where he describes God as pursuing him. He also wrote of his fear that in following God, he would be left with nothing else in his life.

Accepting a call to the priesthood might seem like being wrenched from your family and from the community. Yet many of Richard's family members and those whom he had come to know over the years celebrated with him, shared how he had touched their lives and told of how he had become a treasure to them.

Of all the things said of Richard at his Jubilee, I remember most the quote from Mark Twain, "Kindness is the language which the deaf can hear and the blind can see." His kindness has been evident in his dealings with everyone he has met throughout his life. Surely this trait is why God called Richard to His service and has given him as a special gift to all who have come to know him. Congratulations, Uncle Dick.

Life Lab Lessons

- Think of the kindest person you know.

- Thank God for his or her presence in your life.

- Encourage those who are kind to you by thanking them.

- Think how you could be a little kinder to those who annoy you.

- When someone is kind to you, find a way to pass it on to someone else who needs a touch of kindness.

Keeping Up with Aunt Lucille

People are always blaming their circumstances for what they are. I don't believe in circumstances. The people who get on in this world are the people who get up and look for the circumstances they want, and, if they can't find them, make them.

~G.B. Shaw~

I usually tend to think of older people as relatively immobile, not too interesting in gallivanting, as they call it. But then I am not getting any younger myself. I remember my father retiring and not doing much besides sitting in his lounge chair. Several years ago when I started dating with Carol, I met her Aunt Lucille on one of the few occasions she could be found at home.

My first visit to her house was shortly before Christmas. Carol insisted I see Aunt Lucille's basement. There, amid her husband Jake's clock collection, were more presents that I imagined Santa Claus having in his workshop. She had been chasing around Western New York collecting them for months. I wondered why there was any concern about the economy. During our visit, she was the consummate hostess, seeing to our every need.

Some years later, she was ready to buy a new car and I expressed an interest in her old one. How many miles could an older person put on a car? I was surprised that it had traveled eighty- four thousand miles. I bought the car and named it Lucille in her honor.

Lately she has had medical difficulties which have required her to be tethered to an oxygen tank. I thought this might slow her down some. She has found it inconvenient, but has returned to as much mobility as she can manage within its limitations.

"So what?" you ask. A few years ago when I was struggling with rheumatoid arthritis I had visions of my travels coming to an end or at least being highly curtailed. Aunt Lucille's example reminded me that with determination, quite a bit was possible regardless of circumstances.

Over the years, I have seen many people younger than her, or me for that matter, decide their active lives were over and that it was time to start living on the couch. I grew up in Rochester and have lived in Batavia for many years. During that time I have met quite a few people who were growing older. I have not seen obituaries for most of them, so I assume they are still alive. I wonder what their lives are like.

None of us know how many years we have ahead of us. But that doesn't mean we have to sit still and wait for the end. There is always something we can do today. Aunt Lucille has plans every day, and seems restless if she is not able to get out for at least one adventure.

I have met older people who don't express any opinions and seem not to care much about life. Aunt Lucille knows exactly what she likes and doesn't like with very definite opinions on just about any topic. She has not let life pass her by. Why should we?

Life Lab Lessons

- How well do you use your time each day?
- Do you know someone who makes the most of every day like Aunt Lucille?

- Visit that person and help him or her celebrate life.

- Love the ones you're with.

- Make the best of all your life opportunities.

The Legacy of Our Loved Ones

Death leaves a heartache no one can heal,
love leaves a memory no one can steal.

~From a headstone in Ireland~

Sometimes when people die they leave us money. Sometimes they leave us something more important- part of themselves. We think about our loved ones to keep their memory alive. We share stories of our good times, and lessons we have learned from them while they were alive. Although these memories comfort us in our loss, there is something better we can do. Rather than just treasuring our memories or sharing them with others, we can make them an ongoing part of our lives.

How do we do that? Let's take an example. When we are having a bad day, it's easy to let it show. We might be looking for sympathy from others. In the process we make everyone else's day a little worse. We drag people into our troubles.

Think about loved ones who always had a kind word for everyone no matter what their mood on a particular day. Their challenges that day did not change their cheerfulness toward everyone they met. What if we act the way they did, making a point to share a little joy with everyone no matter how we feel?

If we are in the habit of complaining, doing something different will be a challenge. It will probably be a struggle at first. How would people know we are having a bad day? Does everyone have to know we are having a bad day? Do we really get more sympathy by playing the martyr? Maybe on the surface we do. But think about how you feel about someone who complains all the time. It is a relief when they stop complaining or find someone else to complain to.

Do you have a trait which frequently gets you in trouble or annoys others? Many times we think we are stuck with who we are and can't really change. Maybe the truth is it is too much trouble. We might not know how to go about making changes or what else we can do.

Do you have loved ones in your memory who did not act the way you do now. What they did differently from you? Imagine watching them handle the situation which gets you in trouble. Think about what they would do and at the same time imagine what they would be thinking or feeling. Can you put yourself in their place?

The next time you are in this situation, pretend you are your loved ones. Think their thoughts, take on their feelings and act as they would. In short, be them for a little while. Although strange at first, it might work better for you as well. Maybe you could make it a new habit.

Life Lab Lessons

- Make a list of things about yourself you would like to change.
- Pick one out and think about how your loved one would have handled it.
- Try being that person for a little while.
- See if you feel any different.
- Practice you new behavior.

Goodbye Smokie, We Love You

Don't ask yourself the world needs;
ask yourself what makes you come alive.
And then go and do that.
Because what the world needs
is people who have come alive.

~Harold Whitman~

I saw Smokie about once a year on average over the past eleven years. Yet I was able to share my thoughts, goals and concerns with him in a way I could do with only a few people. We shared observations and opinions about the world, people, and politics among other things. We laughed at others' as well as our own foibles.

He was one of a group of friends who met years ago in Martha's Vineyard and continued to gather in the summer whenever they could. Only once did I have the chance to join him in the Vineyard, his favorite environment. I met him through my life partner, Carol. The two of us were able to travel with him to Scituate, Gloucester, Salem, New Bedford and our favorite destination, Boston.

Carol and I had planned a trip to New Orleans shortly after Smokie retired. He gave us a list of his favorite places to visit and eat and planned to meet us there if his health allowed. Unfortunately he declined and was not able to join us.

Whenever we were in New England, usually on the way to or from his beloved Vineyard, we would visit him but the visits became increasingly challenging. We found him in Massachusetts General Hospital, in an adult home and most recently in a rehabilitation facility.

He declined visits from most of his old friends, maybe because he did not want them to see him deteriorating. He was always glad to see us, however, no matter what condition he was in. We felt fortunate to see him even thought his spirit was slipping away with his body.

Our last visit with him in October was heartbreaking. He was still Smokie but there was not much of him left. In the past an avid traveler and adventurer, he could not move beyond the reach of his oxygen tank, needed a walker and returned from lunch exhausted. My last memory of him was the glint in his eye as we presented him with a blueberry muffin we brought from the Black Dog Bakery on Martha's Vineyard.

Seeing him in that condition was very difficult and we wondered how we could bring ourselves to suffer with him again in his decline. We did not know that would be our last visit with him. He died in November.

A few days ago, forty-six of us who had known Smokie met at his brother-in-law's house in Hanover, close to all Smokie's favorite haunts. We came together to celebrate his life and the ways he had touched each of us. Sitting in a circle, one by one we shared fond memories, stories, and what was special about our relationships with him.

Later we ate together and recalled more stories, both activities Smokie would have loved to share with us. One person noted that those of us who came to remember him that day would probably never be together again. We agreed that we would each take with us the special bonds we had with him and with each other because of him.

I thought maybe he was just special to me. As I listened to all the stories, I realized there was something unique about his spirit and his love of life which we were all fortunate to share. Rest in peace, Smokie.

Life Lab Lessons

- Think of the special people who have touched your life.
- If they are still living, cherish them and let them know you love them.
- If they are no longer living, find a way to honor their memory by the way you live your life.
- Think of your special gifts and how you can share them with those you love.
- Use the gifts from your special people to enrich the lives of those you meet.

Disbursing the Remains of a Life

The world is not to be put in order; the world is order, incarnate.
It is for us to harmonize with this order.

~Henry Miller~

Did you ever wonder about all the objects decorating your life? When you walk through a room in your house or apartment, how often do you notice your furniture, the type of art hanging on your walls or books lining your bookshelves? I suspect not very often.

I wrote above about Lucille. As those of you who knew her realize, she died not too long ago. Recently I attended a house sale where all of her remaining belongings sold briskly. Her relatives divided what they wanted and the rest went on sale. Dolls waving tapers stood in boxes on the lawn with enough other seasonal decorations to furnish a whole block of houses. Once the dolls stood next to the fireplace, the centerpiece among decorations Lucille had gathered over the years.

In the garage, boxes of tools, kitchen gadgets, dishes, picture frames and dress patterns waited for bargain hunters to snatch them up. Browsers surveyed and eventually bought all the furniture and the Lowery organ complete with songbooks.

It occurred to me that as all Lucille's possessions left the premises, they left their stories behind nevermore to be shared. Every Christmas, I remember discussing with her what year one of the dolls had stopped waving its candle and what if anything could be done about it. Then it returned to its box awaiting next year's comments.

Everything in our homes has a story. Some of these stories fascinate one generation after another. Others remain silent for years at a time.

The Source by James Michener remains one of my favorite novels. The story begins with an archeological dig in Israel. A variety of artifacts emerge as excavation progresses. The rest of the novel tells stories associated with each artifact spanning centuries of civilization.

As in every novel, the stories evolved from the author's imagination. Objects separated from their owners lose their meaning. What would an archeologist several thousand years from now make of finding Lucille's eight track player? I dare say it would appear mysterious to many younger people even today.

As I see it, the meaning of our lives does not reside in the possessions we prize while we are alive. After we are gone, the things we left behind don't matter all that much. Seeing Lucille's dresser in Carol's bedroom is not important in itself. What does matter is the wealth of stories it engenders in the memories of those who knew her.

When we meet people, we first notice what they wear, how they present themselves and how they talk. We ask about their jobs, families and pastimes. Maybe we should take more of an interest in the people standing before us rather than the trappings of their lives.

Life Lab Lessons

- Look beyond the superficial in your conversations.
- When you meet someone for the first time ask yourself what might be important to learn.
- Think about how your lives might be similar and different.
- See what you can learn from each other about being human.
- Consider how knowing each person can enrich your life.

Thank You, Michael, for Your Brief Life

Life is to be fortified by many friendships.
To love and to be loved is the greatest happiness of existence.

~Walter Winchell~

Recently I perused the morning paper and found accounts mostly of war, killing and other tragedies. I closed the paper having had my fill of depressing news. In the afternoon paper, I found an article about and obituary for Michael Napoleone. I had recently lost my cherished friend Michael and felt bad for Michael Napoleone's family and many friends. I thought my friend was taken from me too soon but realized my loss paled in comparison with the loss of an eight year old boy.

It is never easy to lose someone you love, especially a child. It defies logic and leaves us feeling cheated. It is easy to think about all that his life could have been had he lived longer. But that was not to be despite his valiant efforts to live and his family's efforts to keep him alive. What does his life mean?

The world is different because of Michael. I felt despair in the morning over all the conflict and aggression in the world. In the afternoon, I felt tears of joy that people could care so much about each other. The caring developed because of Michael, his needs and ability to bring people together around him.

Michael was not a very powerful boy. In contrast he was quite vulnerable. He did not have the power to make anyone do anything but he did have the charisma to bring people together to support him, his family and each other. He gave people a way to work together, to care about each other and to find the strength to come together for a common purpose.

We think of heroes as those who bring people together on a national or international level. Unfortunately, the world has been lacking such a person of late. However we are blessed with people like Michael who bring us together in little ways. The world does not have to change all at once. Coming together in little groups changes it a little at a time.

His family will have their own memories of him, but the rest of us will carry the memory of his courage, joy and appreciation of everything his brief life brought him as examples for our own lives. When we tend to complain about our lives, wish things were different or feel sorry for ourselves, we can remember Michael and how he made the best of each moment. None of us knows how much time we have left. Do we want to spend it wishing it were better or take his example and appreciate all the good things, friends and blessings we have?

Michael leaves us the gift of himself, his acceptance of the life he had and the joy to live each moment to the best of his ability. He invites us to live as he did, accepting life on its own terms. Thank you, Michael.

Life Lab Lessons

- Who have you lost from your life?
- What do you remember best about them?
- What do you treasure most about their memory?
- What would they like you to adopt from their lives?
- When you feel down, live as they would have lived.

Chapter 9

Communication Choices

Some of us are good at expressing our thoughts, some are good listeners and some are good at both. We aren't born good communicators. We have to learn and practice the skill. Do you know when to speak, when to listen and when to appreciate silence?

*****

Hear What You Want to Hear and Disregard the Rest

Reality leaves a lot to the imagination.

~John Lennon~

No, the title of this reflection is not a suggestion but paraphrases a line from the Simon and Garfunkel song, The Boxer. Every time I hear it, I think about context. We don't live in a vacuum and our words don't live in a dictionary. Our environment influences our actions and our relationships form the context of what we say as well as hear.

The first pink hues in the sky don't constitute the whole sunrise nor does the last hint of purple before the sun fully rises. Another example is the story of blind men touching an elephant and drawing very different conclusions about its nature depending on which part of the elephant they were exploring.

For many years, I met with couples locked in the throes of marital problems. Spouses often quoted each other, citing statements their partners had difficulty recognizing as their own. They only heard part of the story. Psychologists have a term for this, selective listening.

Why do we hear only part of what others say? One explanation lies in how we look at life. We tend to pay closer attention to statements which support or radically disagree with our point of view. The rest of the time following a conversation presents more of a challenge. We might lapse into a fog until something relevant sparks our attention.

If we agree with what people say, we compliment them for being right. If we disagree, we berate them for their ignorance. In both cases, we attend better and react more strongly if we consider a statement relevant to our lives and then, as the song says, disregard the rest.

I remember times when I took pains to explain myself carefully only to feel people completely misinterpreted what I said. I thought I should have been clearer in explaining myself. Then I realized they were listening with their ears, mind and experience, not mine. My words registered with them in the context of how they viewed life and not as I viewed it.

So what's the point of all this? To me, it is a reminder to know my audience and how they are likely to hear what I have to say. Of course, that's not always possible. I can't know what other people think, especially before we start talking. My job is to be as clear as possible with my words and listen to their reaction. Then I need to find words which explain what I mean in a way others will understand. We have a choice. We can take insult when others misunderstand us or take responsibility for clarifying what we mean.

Life Lab Lessons

- When was the last time you felt misunderstood?

- Did you clarify what you meant or keep insisting you were right?

- Next time, ask your audience what they heard you say.

- Accept that language is tricky and miscommunication is no one's fault.

- Be patient and try explaining yourself again.

The Myth of Mindreading

Two monologues do not make a dialogue.

~Jeff Daly~

I remember the first story I wrote in high school. I thought it was fine when I handed it in but it was very short. My teacher saw it as sketchy and lacking details. After some thought, I realized that I wrote down only some of what I was thinking. I assumed my readers would know the rest of my thoughts and I was relying on them to be mind readers. I gave my story quite a bit of thought but failed to realize readers could only know what I wrote, not my private thoughts.

The same is true of what we say. Over the years I have come to realize that our words are only a shorthand version and not the context of our thoughts, our emotions and our intentions. On purpose or not, we usually edit our words to include only what we want others to know or sometimes not know.

Not only is there much more to us than the words we share with others, our audience is doing more than just listening to our words. People have their own ideas about most things, and their own ways of making sense of our words. They also have their own hopes, fears and worries. People pay more attention to their own reactions to our words than to what we actually say. They are thinking of what our words mean to them rather than what they mean to us.

No wonder we so often suffer from so much miscommunication and misunderstanding. Communication is more of a transaction than a one way message. Even if our audience is paying attention to us, our words might mean something quite different to them than they do to us. We might be using the wrong words to convey what we want to say. In addition, our tone of voice might convey something different from what our words intend. For example, if we are talking loudly we might just want to be heard. Others might think we are threatening them.

We sometimes expect others to mind read or to understand exactly what we mean, what we intend and how we feel. Later we become angry when we realize that our audience hears something different from what we mean. It is not entirely the responsibility of our audience to understand us.

It is also our responsibility to make sure we are communicating in a way which helps them understand our meaning. We can do this by listening to how our audience reacts to our words. If they react in a way we don't expect, maybe we are not communicating as well as we thought we were. We might need to start over and say our piece in a different way.

Life Lab Lessons

- Notice how people react when you are talking.

- Give your audience a chance to reply to what you say or to ask questions.

- Think about how you can share your feelings rather than assuming others know them.

- Allow others to state their point of view instead of just concentrating on your own.

- Look for areas of agreement rather than stressing the differences.

No Is a Complete Sentence

I cannot give you the formula for success, but I can give you the formula for failure which is: Try to please everybody.

~Herbert B. Swope~

Sometimes the best thing we can say to someone is no. We have focused on understanding others' needs and responding to them the best we can. But we sometimes go overboard meeting other's needs and forget about our own.

We are not machines and do not have endless resources. Sometimes we are exhausted or just tired. We have our own stress. Sometimes we just need to take a break. Codependence is a term from the chemical dependency field which has taken on wider use in our culture. It means going beyond our limits to take care of others, helping them avoid taking responsibility for themselves. In the process, we do harm to ourselves. Another way to put it is being too helpful.

We have physical, mental and emotional limits. Our bodies can do just so much before we become worn out. Mentally, we may not know how to help someone in a given situation. Emotionally, we can become overwhelmed by someone else's needs, leaving us feeling helpless.

Why would someone feel the need to go to such extremes to help others? Some of us have come from families in which our own needs were not met on a physical or emotional level. We may come to see it as our mission in life to meet others' needs at all costs.

Some of us came from families where we had a loved one who continued to struggle with issues such as alcoholism, despite our best efforts to help. Having failed to save our loved one, we may go on to find others to save. This may account for people marrying a series of alcoholic spouses, despite swearing they would never marry someone like their alcoholic parents, or feeling they learned their lesson when their first marriage to an alcoholic failed.

Some of us took on the role of caretaker in our family while we were growing up, seeing it as our job to take care of the rest of the family or to rise to the occasion when anyone needed anything.

Melody Beattie in her book, *The Language of Letting Go,* gives us daily exercises to help us feel okay about ourselves. In another book, *Codependent No More,* she helps us learn that we don't have to depend on others for approval. Our self worth is not dependent on how helpful we are to others. We don't have to overreact to everything in our lives and we don't have to fix everything, especially if we did not break it.

This is not to suggest that we should forget about everyone else and just take care of ourselves. We should look for a balance in our lives, taking care of ourselves first, and then looking at how we can help within the boundaries of our ability. In looking to help others with their needs, we should also consider whether we are capable of helping them, whether they really want or need our help, and whether they will appreciate our efforts.

Life Lab Lessons

- How clear are you in setting limits with others?
- How good are you at accepting others' boundaries?
- Do you know when you efforts are being wasted?
- Can you protect yourself from others taking advantage of you?
- Learn to balance generosity and self protection.

Can You Hear Me Now?

Let us be silent that we may hear the whispers of the gods.

~Ralph Waldo Emerson~

If you watch television at all, you have probably seen a man appearing in the most remote corners of the earth. He stops to make a call on his cell phone asking, "Can you hear me now?" It is possible to stay connected with others no matter where we are. I recently called my brother who lives in Honolulu. He answered his phone standing on a street in Las Vegas.

Even though we can stay in constant touch, is it necessary or even desirable? Due to the danger cell phones present, it was necessary to pass a law banning their use in cars. For a while I did not notice anyone calling while driving. In recent months I have noticed an increase again. A friend of mine told me of a conference she recently attended. Despite a request to turn off cell phones, the speaker was interrupted several times by electronic renditions of various melodies announcing incoming calls.

I don't know what the calls in the cars or at the conference were about. In an airport I overheard people detailing the minute to minute progress of their trips. I am sure some calls are substantial and some even critical. But I have a feeling many are just so people can be engaged in conversation without any particular purpose. Do we really need to be in constant contact with each other?

Another meaning of the word cell occurred to me as I was thinking about this topic. A cell is also the cubicle or room a monk lives in when he is not involved in community activities. In his case, his cell is a place of solitude rather than a means of constant connection with others. Much of my writing has focused on better communication with others. But that doesn't mean we have to engage in it constantly.

Even when we are not on the phone, there is often a radio or TV in the background. What would it be like if we spent some time in silence? We might hear our own thoughts. Maybe we would have a chance to get in touch with our hopes, fears, dreams and wishes. We might have a chance to reflect on our interactions with others, with nature, or with God.

I have suggested to over stimulated people that they turn off all the noise around them and sit in stillness for a while. It is amazing how many people find this prospect uncomfortable.

Plato said, "The unexamined life is not worth living." Without stopping to reflect on our lives, we are like cogs in a machine with no awareness of our place in the larger picture. Some factories take their workers on a tour of the whole assembly line so they can understand the place and importance of their particular contribution.

A period of silence helps us understand how we fit in with those of our fellow life travelers. We have time to gain a sense of the path God has laid out and offered for our acceptance. We also get a better idea of our decisions and their implications. Rather than mindlessly plodding through life, we will be able to make more thoughtful choices.

Life Lab Lessons:

- Do you feel it is important to be in touch with others every minute?

- What would it be like to have a few moments of silence?

- Can you learn to be comfortable with your own thoughts?

- Try tuning into your own thoughts and feelings?

- Learn to enjoy silence.

Listening to the Sound of Silence

Everybody should have his personal sounds to listen for- sounds that will make him exhilarated and alive or quite and calm. One of the greatest sounds of them all-and to me it is a sound- is utter, complete silence.

~Andre Kostelanetz~

I haven't been watching much television lately but I did a few nights ago. Earlier in the evening I survived a breathless used car commercial featuring overlapping shouts. There was no space between sentences and little chance to process anything being said. I think the point was to get people excited about buying a car with no time to consider the decision rationally. Later in the evening I watched a new show about a group of men going to a Benedictine monastery to reassess their lives. They were to spend six weeks there and live as the monks did.

One of the chief features of monastery life is extended periods of silence. The point is for the monks to have time to listen to God and to their own thoughts. The men were invited to try the monastic way of life. When I was younger I spent several years living in a monastery. I found myself thinking back to the times when I had periods of silence built into my daily routine.

I don't think I appreciated silence then. I was young, restless and brash. Silence was a time when I couldn't be doing something useful. There have been many times in my life since then when I have wished to have some silence to gather my thoughts and consider the direction of my life. I had forgotten that I have a choice of how I spent my time that I could choose to have all the silence I wanted. Instead I chose to immerse myself in the cacophony of everyday life.

There is a line from the movie *Cabaret*, "What Good is Sitting Alone in Your Room?" What good is standing in a forest, by the seashore or in a silent snowfall? We all enter this world alone and leave it alone. Silence gives us a chance to keep in touch with the person we are between birth and death. Being alone does not necessarily mean being lonely. The alternative is to rush headlong in whatever direction the crowd is going, even if we are in a pack of lemmings headed for a cliff.

What would it be like if every person in the world took time to be alone? What would happen if everyone listened to their thoughts and then shared them with each other? What if we all listened to each other as we shared our thoughts? Most of us are in a hurry. I wonder how many of us think about where we are headed or what we will do when we reach our destinations.

Life Lab Lessons

- Choose some time today to be with yourself in silence.

- See how hard it is to shut off the outside world.

- See if you can be comfortable just being alone with yourself.

- Listen to hear your dreams, hopes and fears.

- Later tell someone you care about what you learned about yourself.

Joseph G. Langen

Time to Give Words a Rest

The earth is rude, silent, and incomprehensible at first;

Be not discouraged--- keep on---

there are divine things, well envelop'd;

I swear to you there are divine things

more beautiful than words can tell.

~Walt Whitman~

Recently, college and high school students participated in a national Day of Silence to bring attention to anti-LGBT, Lesbian, Gay, Bisexual, Transsexual, name calling, bullying and harassment and effective responses.

Last Sunday, I attended a concert, The Music of Modern American Composers presented by the Genesee Wind Ensemble at Leroy High School. What do these two events have in common? Glad you asked.

Sometimes words interfere with our experience of life. You might think this a strange comment coming from someone who spends most of his time crafting ideas into words. Sometimes I feel bombarded by words and wish they would just go away, at least for a while.

On Sunday I had a chance to sit for a time without words interfering. Wind instruments meditated, reflected and exploded into melodies while percussion instruments punctuated the woodwind airs. Sometimes they raced to keep up with each other. A rendition of Shenandoah begged for its familiar words. I managed to content myself with humming along rather than singing out loud. Moods, feelings and visceral experience took hold of me without a single word uttered. Later, I could only say I enjoyed the concert but couldn't put my experience into words. I guess that's not surprising.

I read about the Day of Silence but had no campus handy where I could experience the event. I know reading about it is not the same as being there. Yet, to me, silence more eloquently portrayed the difficulties and challenges of LGBT students than any words could.

Many years ago I lived in a monastery and experienced on a daily basis the volumes silence speaks. A picture is worth a thousand words. How many written and spoken words over the centuries have tried to describe the human experience- its emotions, trials and joys? Much remains unsaid. To some extent, words cannot do justice to our common life story.

When lost for words about a particular topic, I am fond of chalking it up to being just one of life's mysteries. I have experienced many an event, feeling or encounter for which words fail me. How do you describe a Hawaiian sunset?

Words can also crush us. It's easy to say, "Sticks and stones my break my bones, but names will never hurt me." Living this statement becomes much more difficult when taunts come our way accompanied by derisive laughter. How many times do we lash out at others we see as beneath us or maybe just different from us. Maybe we are expressing our fears, insecurities and hurts for which we have no adequate words. What if we take some time to experience our feelings without labeling them? Perhaps then we can use our words more constructively the next time our feelings show up.

Life Lab Lessons

- Choose some time to be silent for a while.

- Make an effort to shut off the words in your mind.

- See what feelings float around inside you.

- Let them be there without comment or labels.

- Now think about how you can best express yourself and your feelings.

Chapter 10

Valuing Our Relationships

The best thing about being human is that we don't have to live
life alone. We have others with whom to share our life journey.
Some people were there waiting for us to be born. Others pass
through our lives daily. We have the choice of which of our
companions to treasure. Choose wisely.

*****

Challenge Yourself to Share Your Love

You don't choose your family.
They are God's gift to you, as you are to them.

~Desmond Tutu~

Morals used to mean principles by which people lived. They
were ways to make sense of the world, ourselves and our
relationships. Morality was a word bandied about in this year's
election, but what does it really mean? I remember hearing a fair
amount of talk about family values during the campaign without
much explanation of any particulars.

When I listened closer, I did not hear much about what families,
parents or children should do. Most of the focus was on what
people should not do, such as abortion and gay marriage. This
position implied that outlawing such practices would improve
the quality of family life.

Even in families which profess strong adherence to a religion, there is still significant difficulty with infidelity, divorce, alcoholism, abuse and other problems. It does not appear that religious affiliation will always assure family harmony.

While the bible documents humanity's struggle to come to terms with itself and with God, passages from the Bible have been used to justify genocide, war and many other destructive acts. It seems all too easy to forget there is a God who loves us all equally. Sometimes we are tempted to think we have special favor in God's eyes and others are lesser beings.

Over the years, many religions have become institutionalized and fearful of growth. The end result can be a rigid set of rules, commanding what believers can and cannot do. At times, it seems there is more concern about the rules than about finding God. Some people appreciate a well defined path to salvation, absolving them of having to think about their path. Others have challenged tradition and forged their own way to God, sometimes being shunned or even executed for their efforts.

In the biblical story of the Magi, we learn about three wise men following a star in the heaven, avoiding entanglement in political intrigue and discovering Jesus, surrounded by animals and shepherds. There is something peaceful about this scene transcending traditional religions.

While moral guideposts can be helpful, we also need to look into our own hearts to see what lies there. What is important to us? Are we using the gifts God has given us to improve our lives and those of others whose lives we touch? Are we living what we believe instead of just professing our beliefs?

Spirituality transcends religion and connects us with God as well as with each other. In O Henry's story, The Gift of the Magi, two spouses gave up their most precious possessions to enhance each other's lives. It turned out that the things they gave up for themselves and bought for each other were less important than the love behind their choices. Our love for each other is the greatest gift God has given us. It is up to us to find ways we can share this gift with each other.

Life Lab Lessons

- What does family mean to you?

- Do you think of family rules or family love?

- Do you think some people are more deserving of love than others?

- How do you decide this?

- Would feeling loved change a person for the better?

Loving in the Shadow of Cancer

Love is a force more formidable than any other. It is invisible- it cannot be seen or measured, yet it is powerful enough to transform you in a moment, and offer you more joy than any material possession could.

~Barbara De Angelis~

St. Paul wrote to the Corinthians, "Love is always patient, love is always kind." We hear these words most often in wedding ceremonies. Loving is easy at this special moment and other times of celebration for lovers.

How hard is it to be patient when everything falls into place? How hard is it to be kind when life treats you well? Unfortunately life is not always generous or accommodating. Sometimes it is very difficult and threatens to disrupt or destroy the relationships which make our lives worth living.

Cancer sometimes unravels the body piece by piece, stripping off former skills and even basic abilities. At other times it provides a brief scare but no real interference with life as we know it. It can also cause a major disruption but after treatment allow us to go on as before. Ultimately it can change the course of life irrevocably.

Recently I had the privilege of spending some time with my friends Kat and Paula. I saw the power of cancer but also its limits. Cancer undermines Kat's stamina, balance and concentration. However it is powerless to shake their love and

145

can't stop them from expressing it in kisses, embraces and loving glances. I thought of the line from Michael Row the Boat Ashore, "The River Jordan is chilly and cold. Chills the body but not the soul." Their love shines through the strain of cancer and remains stronger than anything it can throw at them.

Eighteen years together has prepared their love for each other to withstand the onslaught of one of the worst trials I can imagine. In the face of extreme stress, beyond what many of us will ever face, their affection radiates love at a level I have seldom seen in any relationship, particularly under the circumstances which face them.

Cancer seems to take over the lives of those it affects and we appear to be at its mercy. But we do have choices. We can allow cancer to take its course or we can accept medical treatment, alternative care or both. We can give up on life or continue to live it fully each day.

Cancer provides a serious challenge to the love of those whom it affects. If we give in to its onslaught, it can destroy our relationships. If we rise to the challenge we can deepen our ties to a point beyond the reach of cancer or of any other misfortune.

Life Lab Lessons

- What adversities do you face in your relationships?
- How have you handled adversity in the past?
- What joys do you share with those you love?
- Have you relished these joys with them?
- How can you use your love, patience and kindness to overcome your trials together?

What Are Friends For?

I value the friend who for me finds time on his calendar, but I cherish the friend who for me does not consult his calendar.

~Robert Brault~

I was thinking the other day that we tend to take friends for granted. We expect them to be there when we need them, to understand us and support our efforts.

I realized that all friends are not the same. We have acquaintances whom we greet when we see them. We usually know each other by name, briefly comment on the weather, sports or other shared interests and go on about our business.

Another group of friends consists of people with whom we may go to events, share tools or help out with major projects. They are not in our lives on a constant basis but seem to show up when needed, sometimes without being asked. We expect these friends to be aware of our needs and help out when they can. We do the same for them. We tend to be offended if they ignore our needs.

We have close friends who know more about us. We share with them the major struggles in our lives and expect them to know how we feel about most things. Even if our opinions do not agree, we expect them to respect what we think, as we do for them.

There is another level of friendship whose members have come to be known as soul mates. They know us better than we know ourselves. They can act as our conscience and can tell us things which would cause offense if we heard them from someone else. They are almost part of us and can sense what we think or feel.

These four types of friendship develop from acquaintanceship to deeper relationships over time if we let them. Some people don't allow themselves to have many acquaintances, if any. They routinely ignore others' attempts to share a friendly hello and make it clear that they do not want to share their lives with anyone. After a while people stop making the effort and leave them to their isolation.

We can return friendly chatter and keep our involvement at that level. Or we can begin to share some of ourselves and take an interest in others in return. As we discover what we have in common, interests grow and deepen. Again we have a choice of how much we are willing to share.

As we get to know and trust casual friends, they may eventually join the circle of our close friends. We know they will be there for us when we have a major crisis and we are there for theirs as well. We share deeply in each other's joys and sorrows and sometimes seem like part of each other's families.

Soul mates do not seem to be chosen. I don't think we pick people out at any of the three previous stages and decide we would like them as soul mates. It just happens over time. It is almost as if we allow these people into our brains and emotional centers so that they become part of us. I don't think everyone has a soul mate.

Many people are not comfortable sharing enough of themselves to allow this level of intimacy. No matter how many friends we have, it is our job to treasure them and let them know we appreciate them, as well as being there for them when they need us.

Life Lab Lessons

- What do you expect from your friends?
- Are your expectations realistic?
- Do you expect more from your friends than you are willing to give?
- Do your offer your friends the best you have?
- Let your friends know how much you treasure them.

What It Takes to Stay Married for Sixty Years

A good marriage is like a good trade:
Each thinks he got the better deal.

~Ivern Ball~

Last Saturday night, I was invited to celebrate the eightieth birthday of Rose VanValkenburg. The same party celebrated sixty years of marriage to her husband Russ. I thought about how many marriages don't last very long at all and how more marriages fail than succeed. Most people include the words until death do us part in their wedding vows and I think most of them intend to stay together until the end.

Yet that isn't the reality. I tried to think of all the reasons marriages fail but keep ending up with lists of reasons which sound hollow and superficial. Maybe I was asking the wrong question. I decided to word it differently this time. How did Rose and Russ manage to stay married all these years? I asked them.

Rose was succinct. Her first challenge was to keep her mouth shut. Complaining about everything she disliked would not get her anywhere except into the midst of hard feelings and resentments. Second was to stress on the positive. If she keeps her mind and energy focused on what she likes, she has a much better chance of having a happy life. Third, live each day for itself. There is nothing to be gained by regretting the past or worrying about the future. Today is the only one she can do anything about.

Russ could not tell me what kept their marriage together except that there were many things. He was more eloquent when writing his feelings, "Without Rose, I could not have accomplished only about one half of what I did. Rose has been my best friend, my helper, my cook, my maid, my lover and a darn good nurse whenever I was sick. What more could a man ask for in marriage?"

His appreciation of all his wife has done for him over the years was his answer. When we take our partners for granted, we let go of the magic which binds us and makes our lives joyous and worth living.

Rose's cousin Renee summarized the feelings of the family and the rest of us:

> Love is kind, caring and sincere,
>
> Love takes more selflessness than anything,
>
> Love is sharing and giving.
>
> Love is meeting the needs of others,
>
> Love is unconditional.
>
> Your love and compassion shine
>
> light in every room you enter.

Love still shines bright in both of your eyes.

Love takes no less than everything

Of your heart and soul.

A love greater than yours is only

The love that God gives to his children.

Your love has been portrayed as husband and wife,

Mother and father,

Grandparents and extended family.

There is no other love as warm,

No better example besides the love of God that we can think of.

You are love, kindness, laughter,

Charm, warmth, compassion, advisors,

And nurturers of man and animal.

That's what you are to us.

What an example to follow.

What a blessing it is to have both

Of you in our lives.

Sticks and Stones May Break Our Bones

Have patience awhile; slanders are not long-lived. Truth is the child of time; ere long she shall appear to vindicate thee.

~Immanuel Kant~

The realization that many of us have joined company with our government in conducting our affairs on borrowed money prompted a reflection we will get to later. Recently I became aware of another parallel, one between political candidates and aspiring college students.

Candidates have often followed a pattern of promising to run their campaigns focusing on the issues. When it comes to brass tacks, the gloves come off and the political ads become ugly. Jodi Cohen recently reported in a Chicago Tribune article that some high school seniors and their parents have taken to sending anonymous letters to prospective colleges. The letters served to sling mud at other applicants in an attempt to reduce competition for college freshman slots.

What do these observations say about our political system and students who want to better themselves at others' expense? We like to think of ourselves as living in a civilized society. Trampling on others to get what we want is obviously not very civilized. To my way of thinking, such behavior suggests that its perpetrators are unsure of themselves. They don't feel they accomplish enough on their own merits. Desperate measures indeed.

Perhaps some people seek positions for which they are unqualified. If they can make the competition look bad, their own chance of getting what they want improves.

What does this behavior do to our society? One effect is to undermine our trust in each other. Expecting lies, distortions or having our shortcomings publicly displayed makes the rest of us more cautious about what we reveal to others. Even if we don't have any significant shortcomings, putting ourselves in the public eye risks attack by those who find our words threatening to them in some way. If good people are afraid to take such risks, more opportunity remains for those with flexible morals. What can society expect of these individuals once they get what they want?

So what's the alternative? Unfortunately, no one is in charge of deciding how we should live constructively in society. In our country, freedom of speech remains one of our basic rights. We have legal sanctions for libel and slander but rumors are often perpetuated with few consequences.

That leaves it up to us to develop a society where we are more respectful of each other and accept others' greater skills and qualifications without resorting to dirty tricks. Society doesn't change by itself. It changes only when its citizens change. It is up to us to change our own lives and relationships. These personal strides will eventually result in a different society. We have limited power as individuals but, when we all start acting more responsible, we will find ourselves living in a world where we can feel better about each other as well as about ourselves.

Life Lab Lessons

- How do you react to attacks on another's character?
- Do you pass on the attacks in your conversations?
- Is what you say about others true?
- Is what you say kind?
- Do your words about others serve a constructive purpose?

Love the Ones You're With

If you can't be with the one you love, love the one you're with.

~Stephen Stills~

Michael, an entertainer I know, travels the world on a cruise ship. Every time his mother e-mails him, she ends by writing, "Love the ones you're with."

Years ago, we were surrounded by the ones we loved. Generations of families were born, raised, lived and died in the same neighborhood. These days, it is uncommon to live near those who are most important to us. Families and friends are left behind as we seek our fortunes wherever they may lie.

We often find ourselves among strangers, at least until we get to know them. They don't know where we came from, what our family traditions are or what is important to us. We leave our roots when we move from our old environment. Like transplanted trees, we may be in shock for a while and look a little withered.

We can stay isolated in our new environment and try to survive without the support we once had in our previous surroundings. Without finding new sources of support, life may become lonely. There is no one to verify our efforts, listen to our plans, cheer us or console us.

We might have a family to move with us. However family members all tend to be quite busy and preoccupied with their own activities these days. Our spouses or life partners hopefully are the ones with whom we share our love and whose love we receive in return. Our parents are ahead of us in our life journey and our children behind us.

Love the ones you're with. We meet fellow life travelers at work, at the gym, church, the library, and other places around town. But we don't love people we have just met. We don't know them well enough. Sometimes we think of love as the romantic attachments which form the basis of movies, novels and songs. I am referring here to another type of love which involves knowing what another's life is about and helping that person live the best life he or she can.

This is not to say that we take responsibility for the course of another's life. Taking too much responsibility is almost as bad as not being helpful at all. There are many small ways we can love those we are with. They consist of the small kindnesses we show each other, the interest we take in each other's lives and sharing what we have learned from our experience which might be helpful to others in living their lives.

We often don't choose the ones we're with. Often they come with the work or social activities we choose. I remember taking pains to greet a street vendor in Spain with the meager Spanish at my command. Although I will probably never see him again, he explained a little about his life and the Reconquista celebration going on in his town of Vigo that day. I ended up being greatly enriched by my small effort.

We have frequent opportunities to love the ones we're with. Making the effort may be rewarding in ways we least expect.

Life Lab Lessons

- As a child, did you think your relatives would always be there in your life?

- What was it like if you moved away from people you loved and who loved you?

- How easy is it for you to make new friends?

- Do you tend to hibernate instead?

- Relish the opportunity to meet new people and form new relationships.

Customer Satisfaction

It really becomes a problem for us on customer satisfaction.

~Phil Wright~

Dear Owner,

I wasn't clear whether the customer satisfaction survey I found on the table in the cottage was meant for me to fill out. It was difficult to see how it could do justice to our experience with you over the past week. However it did give me the idea that some feedback regarding our week here might be useful to you.

I must confess that I wondered why your cottage was the only one on either side of Conesus Lake that had a for rent sign in front. The lake has long been very popular. Last year we had to reserve a cottage six months in advance. This year we could not get the same cottage back even with eight months notice.

Your arrangements seemed a little unusual. We have never stayed in a cottage where the owner stayed on the same property. However I guess that having two cottages back to back on the same property does solve the problem of whether you want to use your cottage or rent it out. You can do both.

We were surprised when we arrived to see you sitting in the living room working on the front door lock. Your still being there two hours later and the lock still not working made us wonder whether you were really working on it or just wanted to see what we were bringing into the cottage. It felt just the tiniest bit intrusive, but then why be paranoid on vacation?

We were glad when you finally left, but found it inconvenient to have to drag everything in through the back hall over your water jugs and boxes. I guess there are always some small inconveniences in roughing it.

We had thought about having a sailboat last year, but no one in the family had one and there were none for rent at the marina. My sister and my brother's girl friend were therefore initially pleased when you pointed out your Sunfish to them, even though it accommodated only two. They were both ready to take it for a ride when it became clear that you were talking about going out with each of them one at a time. It was difficult to hear what your wife said as you returned to your cottage disappointed about their disinterest in sailing with you. However from her gestures it looked like this was not the first time you proposed such an idea to guests.

There was one positive outcome from this encounter, although it might not have happened if you had all of your teeth in when you grinned at the women. Later that night, when we were playing Scattergories, everyone was struggling with movie titles beginning with D. Neither of the women had any trouble thinking of Deliverance.

Those of us who tended to sleep late were somewhat concerned about the thin gauze curtains and wished there was something more substantial on the windows. We were aware from page six of the rules that you had a limit on the number of guests who could stay overnight. We figured you did not want hundreds of people sleeping all over the place. However we never thought you meant this limit literally, and certainly never expected you would come around to look in each window during the night and count how many people there were. Other than that, we slept pretty well except for your waking us up at 2:30 AM when you went down cellar, which was also within your rights as provided for on page 22.

Regarding the bathroom, we did have some prior experience with septic systems. I must say your list of what not to put in the toilet was complete. No sanitary napkins, tampons, disposable diapers, feminine hygiene towlettes, condoms or wrappers, contraceptive sponges, disposable enemas or douches or containers for either, or used caches sexe.

I have to admit you almost had me on the last one. If I had not read Gary Jennings Spangle last winter, I would not have known that a cache sexe was a kind of codpiece that circus performers wore. Was this your attempt at humor, or do you regularly have acrobats staying here?

I have learned that most people do not like to be nagged, especially on vacation. I was thinking there is a way you might be able to protect your plumbing with a sign which is at once succinct, direct and positive. What would you think of, "Urinate, defecate, terminate?"

The reason we came to a cottage was to be near the water. The beach front was fairly adequate for a few people. We did understand from page eight that your family was to be allowed access to the beach front. We thought you meant your wife, two children and yourself. We were therefore more than a little surprised when Alfred, your second cousin once removed, his four grown children, their spouses and children arrived in early afternoon one day and stayed until dusk. Since the children in our family are all grown, we did not expect to spend the afternoon wiping noses and changing diapers. However, I suppose it was somewhat nostalgic.

It was the waterfront itself we had trouble understanding. It was convenient to have a dock in front of the cottage, although we realized from page twelve of the regulations that we could not attach our boat to it. We expected to use it for loading and unloading. We were, however, mildly inconvenienced by the aforementioned Sunfish which you anchored several feet off the dock with the sail tied upright. With the wind blowing from the North, as it was on Wednesday, it was not possible to see the dock from the lake much less reach it.

We had not realized there were so many ways to interrupt people trying to water ski. My brother thought your snorkeling between the boat and skier as they were making preparations was most ingenious although my sister thought wind-surfing in the same spot was also quite creative. Don't you think either activity might have been dangerous with tenants less patient than we were?

We did find it inconvenient to move our cars each time you decided to attack a different tree along the driveway with a pruning saw. However, we did not realize this was just a prelude to the final act. We thought it might be nice to sit by the water the last afternoon and evening. We got to relax for about fifteen minutes.

Everyone confessed to being amazed that an accountant like you would have such an outfit. At first, we thought, with all the leather straps you were wearing, you and your wife had a kinky afternoon tryst planned. But when we saw the lineman spikes you were wearing and the chain saw in your hand it was hard to imagine your getup was entirely for your wife's benefit.

We tried to ignore you, but it was hard not to notice when you fired up the chain saw and started climbing the linden tree. Some discussion of your intentions may have been helpful beyond your simply yelling timber. It was thoughtful of you to attack the tree on the right side of the yard while we were sitting on the left to catch the afternoon sun. Still, some of the branches fell a little too close for comfort.

Did you notice the large wasp nest on one of the limbs you trimmed? We certainly did as it hit the ground and the wasps headed in our direction, taking us as the impetus for their untimely descent.

We managed to get to the cottage and inside with a minimum of stings. The swarm did not give up easily and buzzed around the screens, intent on revenge. They eventually found an entrance and chased us around the cottage.

You may have wondered where we had gone, why we were not in our beds at night and why we did not check out until 11:00 AM rather than 10:00 AM per page 42. The truth is we were not able to get the exterminator to come until 10:30 so we could get back in to retrieve out belongings. Under the circumstances I think it only proper that you return our security deposit. Credit for the last night would certainly not be out of the question either.

There are two final questions on the survey. One is how we would rate our overall satisfaction with our stay. No thoughts devoid of expletives come to mind. The final question is whether we would be interested in coming back next summer. I think we will look for some place on Seneca Lake next year unless you happen to own property there as well.

Life Lab Lessons

Draw your own.

Chapter 11

Appreciating People's Differences

Our lives would be boring if we were all the same. Fortunately people come in many varieties. Sometimes it's not so easy to accept people thinking, feeling and acting in ways different from ours. But it's much easier to make sense of the world if we do. Try it if you haven't.

*****

Navigating the World of Stigma

Mental illness is nothing to be ashamed of,
but stigma and bias shame us all.

~Bill Clinton~

The word stigma comes from the Greek for "mark". Greek citizens cut or tattooed signs or marks on people to show they were slaves, criminals or traitors to be avoided in common society. The Jewish star worn in Nazi Germany indicated the lower status of a whole race of people. In the story The Scarlet Letter, Nathanial Hawthorne has Hester Prynne wearing a scarlet "A" on her clothing to warn others that she is to be shunned as an adulteress. On a more positive note, mystics through the ages developed stigmata, the marks of Jesus' wounds, inviting reflection on his life and suffering.

For the most part, a stigma is a sign of lower social standing. More important, a stigma is not so much a sign of personal character as an indication of how we should treat the person who has the stigma. We consider "us" as normal while we consider "them" as abnormal or inferior. Stigma is a way to identify others we hold in lower regard.

We tend to find imperfections in others who are not up to our standards and are not seen as being as good as we are. This is not much different from the desperate search in junior high school to feel better about oneself by finding something to make fun of in others.

Everybody wants to be normal and no one wants to be left out. I learned in graduate school that normal is just another word for average. There is nothing special about being normal. It is just a way to hide in the crowd and not be noticed.

Is there anyone who is actually normal? Each of us is different in some way from everyone else on earth. Some of our unique traits, along with their signs or stigmata, are more obvious than others. Some are evident from a distance while others are not so obvious until we get closer.

Some differences don't matter at all if we don't have to deal with the people who have them. Actually we can find those different from us rather fascinating until it comes time to interact with them on a personal basis. Hence circus side shows.

Our fears, ignorance and prejudices can make us uncomfortable and awkward in our encounters. Have you ever found yourself taking louder to a blind person or trying to reason with an intoxicated person? If we don't understand the person's differences, we won't know how to interact effectively.

Instead we look for signs of difference warning us to keep our distance so we don't have to trouble ourselves. The problem is that we all have our differences as well as signs, or stigmata, telling others of our differences. If each of us avoided everyone different from us, we would have no one else to talk with. It is a challenge to navigate our neighbors'' differences, but they are what make the world such an interesting place in which to live.

Life Lab Lessons

- Think about how you identify people different from you.

- How does this difference affect your dealings with that person?

- What makes you unique?

- In what way does your difference change how people deal with you?

- Think about how it would change your relationships if you understood others' differences and they understood yours?

A Few More Thoughts on Stigma

*A great many people think they are thinking
when they are merely rearranging their prejudices.*

~Edward R. Murrow~

Stigma is not an easy topic to think, read, talk or write about. If there is something different about us, we would prefer that no one notice or comment on it. If there are imperfections in those we meet, we expect them to accept their inferiority and defer to us.

Some stigmas are more obvious than others. Physical disability, skin color and odd behavior are all quite easy to see. Such stigmas immediately set off those who possess them as different from us "normal" people.

There are other stigmas which are not so easy to spot. Mental illness, lower intelligence, sexual orientation and some diseases might remain hidden for some time. If we knew about these stigmas, we would treat their owners different from those who, like ourselves, don't have them.

Most of us seem to have a natural tendency to want to be the best. Unfortunately, many of us take it a step further and want to be sure we are better than the average person, or even better than everyone else. Stigmas can be handy ways to demote the competition, giving us a rating system to rank ourselves higher and to rank them lower compared with us. Stigmas can also be ways to bunch people into convenient groups according to our stereotypes and prejudices so we don't have to give them any more thought. Oh, he's just crazy.

We often don't want to be bothered taking the time to understand those around us, especially those we label as different or inferior. We would be just as happy to let them stay in their place and keep out of our way. In one sense, this does make our lives a little easier but also means we have to work harder to be sure our lives are not affected by undesirables.

What happens when we spend our time making sure we are better than others? We see what's wrong with everyone but ourselves. There are things about each of us that could use some attention. But we will never see shortcomings if we are always busy noting others' faults. If we stop to think about it, we will realize that we are the only ones we can change. We can't make any one else different.

We can understand what it is like for others to live their lives. We can learn lessons from their struggles to help us with our own. Our acceptance of others' differences will make it easier for them to accept ours. Other people will be more likely to accept us at face value if we accept them as they are.

Life Lab Lessons

- What one stigma in others makes you most uncomfortable?

- Try to figure out what makes you uncomfortable about it.

- If you don't know much about this stigma, see what you can find out about it.

- Think what it would be like for you to carry a stigma.

- The next time you meet someone with a stigma, see if you are still as uncomfortable.

Watching People Walk Out of a Performance

If men would consider not so much where they differ,
as wherein they agree, there would be far less
of uncharitableness and angry feeling in the world.

~Joseph Addison~

At the Rochester International Jazz Festival I had the opportunity to hear music I have never heard before and instruments I could not have imagined. One instrument sat behind a piano. I can still only imagine what it looked like. The sounds reaching my ears seldom evoked a sense of familiarity. I had no way to categorize what I heard or relate it to anything familiar. Even though much of the music sounded strange to my ear, whatever reached me from the stage grabbed my attention.

I must admit it is easier for me to listen to familiar favorites than unfamiliar music. They don't require any work from me. I just sit back, relax and enjoy them. That night I knew I was in for a challenge. I was ready for something new as were a few other brave souls. They had also arrived to hear a mix of American Jazz and African Rhythm. Or so I thought.

The first selection set the tone for the evening. The meager audience survived it intact. At the last note, a handful of people rose and made their way toward the exits. I thought they must have been confused somehow about the nature of the concert. After almost every subsequent number, another handful, sometimes more, beat a hasty retreat. After I while I feared I might be one of only a few remaining stragglers still in their seats.

I thought back to my college years when I tried attending performances with a companion who invariably walked out of each musical performance, lecture or reading we attended. I kept trying to find something she liked, but she kept walking out.

I don't remember a time when I ever walked out of a performance no matter how much it grated against my expectations. Maybe there's something odd about me. On the way home that night, I thought about what it must be like for entertainers to see their audience give up on them. In most cases, performers of my acquaintance appear to share their talent and their views of the world from whatever perspective they have. To my mind, walking out of a show insults their efforts.

I wondered if there could be a performance which I would abandon. I might if I thought the performer was insulting the audience, making no effort to connect with them or was blatantly incompetent. Even then, I might be tempted to wait around to see if any chance of redemption occurred.

Am I too accepting? Maybe, but I tend to give everyone the chance I would like to receive if I were in their shoes. Even if I didn't do a great job, I would like people to hear me out and then tell me what I might improve the next time.

Life Lab Lessons

- Do you approach new situations with an open mind?
- If not, what part of you does something new threaten?
- Do you realize that if you're not growing, you're dying?
- How does a new experience upset your balance?
- Try something you have never done before and see what you can learn from it.

What Happened to Respect?

I'm not concerned with your liking or disliking me.
All I ask is that you respect me as a human being.

~Jackie Robinson~

On the surface, it seems life has become a free for all. It looks like it is every person for him or herself. Financially, our goal is to grab what we can. In our relationships, the guiding principle is, "Get out of my way!"

Internationally, our country is seen as wanting to impose its will on the rest of the world. Historically, powers which have dominated large regions of the world have had their way, sometimes for centuries, but have eventually faded into oblivion or relative obscurity.

We have been blessed in our country with wonderful natural resources. We have traditionally been a melting pot incorporating the contributions of many different peoples. We have developed the technology to help us become very powerful. Sometimes we are aware of our blessings but do we always remember the obligations which go with them?

The French have a saying: "Noblesse oblige- nobility has its obligations." There has always been a tendency of civilizations and well off citizens to drift toward abuse of wealth and power, as well as sometimes using it for the common good of civilization.

Pierre Teilhard De Chardin in *The Phenomenon of Man* and Thomas Berry in *The Dream of the Earth* and in *The Great Work* predicted and hoped for a world movement beyond political and religious conflict where we could reconnect with our fellow humans and with the earth. They foresee our development of a respect for each other and for the tremendous resources we have at our disposal. They expect a time when we will learn to use our differences to discover what is missing in our own lives and find ways to preserve, rather than plunder and waste, the resources at our disposal.

All of this seems like a tremendous challenge and a long trek from our current world situation. Respect for each other and for the earth needs to begin with respect for ourselves. This is easier said than done. How do we do it?

Have you ever noticed the sense of wonderment children have at discovering an animal, the ocean or even the toes at the end of their feet? Somehow, as we get older, we lose this sense of wonderment and start taking things for granted. How wonderful is children's art before they learn there are rules for painting?

We can take time out from our bustle to reflect on what we have, even if it is only a tenuous grip on life. We need to appreciate the beauty which surrounds us in nature and learn to enjoy the company we have on the path toward making sense of our lives. We can appreciate and learn to respect our place in the world, the world itself, and those who inhabit it with us. Put in this perspective, we can learn to share our path through life with our fellow travelers and also leave a well tended path for those who will follow us.

Life Lab Lessons

- Do you expect others to respect you?

- Do you respect others as much as you expect them to respect you?

- Do you think your children will respect you if you don't respect them?

- What could we as a world community accomplish with mutual respect?

- Try it.

Listening to the Voices in Your Head

Prayer is when you talk to God.
Meditation is when you listen to God.

~Author Unknown~

Many years ago I was walking in a monastery garden and stopped a priest to share my latest concerns with him. Rather than becoming caught up in my dilemma of the moment, he took thought a moment, took a deep breath and then he said, "I hear you talking, Brother."

I wasn't sure what to make of his reply but have thought about it off and on over the years. He heard me and I had a sense that he understood me, but he was not about to let my musings upset him. I had to stop my worrying for a while to wonder what his reply meant.

This morning I was reading Eckhart Tolle's book, *The Power of Now*. Thanks for or the suggestion, Bob. He writes about the constant stream of monologues and dialogs taking place all the time in our minds. You don't have to be mentally ill to hear voices. We all do, but most of us keep them to ourselves. Whether or not we believe in ghosts, words are flying at us all the time. The voices are louder some times than they are at other times, but they are always there chattering away.

Sometimes we let the voices take over our awareness. We become one with their messages of anger, fear, uncertainty or whatever other emotions they want to foist upon us. We get lost trying to make sense of everything that has happened in our past and trying to plan for the future. The past and future provide a context for our lives but we only live in the present moment.

Tolle reminds us that the only reality we have is right now. We can't change the past. We can't control the future. Did you ever ruin your present moment by fretting over the past or trying to plan a perfect way to handle something which has not yet happened and might never happen?

Tolle talks about separating ourselves from our thoughts and feelings. Monks take vows of poverty, chastity and obedience to detach themselves from earthly concerns so they can focus on their relationship with God. Probably more important than putting aside earthly concerns is detachment from the thoughts and feelings wrestling for control of our souls.

Do you remember a time when you were able to set aside your voices and all their concerns? Could you just enjoy being yourself as part of the universe? Do you remember how this happened and what it felt like? You might find you like being in this space even for a little while.

Life Lab Lessons:

- What would it be like to listen to the voices in your head but not take them seriously or even quiet them altogether for a time?

- If you have been able to be alone and at peace with yourself, what difference did it make in your life?

- If you have had this experience how could you recreate it?

- Where would it be easiest to do this: in the woods, on the shore of a lake or ocean, in a garden?

- Do you think you would benefit from trying it again?

The Stigma of Mental Illness

The imposition of stigma is the commonest form of violence used in democratic societies.

~R.A. Pinker~

At a recent annual meeting of the Mental Health Association in Batavia, NY, the speaker, George Roets, and several of the artists on the panel mentioned the stigma associated with mental illness. They talked about the negative image which people with mental illness share, as well as the fear of mental illness common in our culture.

A stigmatized person may bring about feelings of awkwardness, discomfort, fear or misunderstanding in others. Most of these feelings come from seeing a condition rather than the person who has it. These feelings come from prejudice and judging people for their condition rather than for who they are. Behind every stigma is a person with fears, hopes, dreams, wants and needs.

Some stigmata are quite obvious. It is hard to miss a person with blindness, cerebral palsy or crippling arthritis. Some are more difficult to notice on the surface, such as deafness, diabetes or mental illness. The words mental illness can themselves be a stigma. Carrying the stigma of mental illness and facing others' discomfort with it usually makes people feel worse than they already do for just having such a condition. It also makes a person careful about revealing the mental illness to others for fear of becoming a social outcast or not being considered for a job.

What else does the stigma of mental illness mean? People with this label have had to work harder than most others just to survive in the world. They have had to wrestle with the workings of their mind which many people take for granted. They have had to learn to find their strengths despite struggling with their own inner demons. They have had to accept their problems with their thoughts and emotions, sometimes far beyond what other have had to face.

Life with mental illness is not easy, but it is possible to become stable, productive and self sufficient. The artists at the annual meeting have shown us that it is also possible to go beyond survival and create something special, surpassing the capabilities of many people.

Their stigma comes partially from their mental illness. However their mark is on canvas, paper or metal, ready to be shared with others and gives others a glimpse into their lives. Their art also gives viewers a chance to consider their own lives and learn to understand themselves a little better.

Life Lab Lessons

- What would it be like for you to be mentally ill?

- How would you expect others to approach you if they did at all?

- Think of times you may have experienced temporary craziness.

- Think about the closeness of creativity and madness.

- Try to set aside your prejudices.

Mental Illness- Relatively Speaking

The patient should be made to understand that he or she must take charge of his own life. Don't take your body to the doctor as if he were a repair shop.

~Quentin Regeste~

When our children are born we see them as miracles, little bundles of life for which all things are possible. We have dreams for them, sometimes hoping they can do the things we have not been able to do in life, sometimes imagining them going on to do great things in the world, and always imagining them as being successful no matter what they attempt.

We don't think about the difficulties they will face, imagining we can protect them from the troubles we have faced in our own lives. We forget that we have gained our emotional strength from learning to deal with the adversities life has in store for all of us. We imagine our children will be exempt from hard times. We become angry and defensive at the thought that we might not be able to protect our children from harm.

Somehow it is easier to accept physical injury or illness in our children than mental problems. It still upsets us, angers and disappoints us, but somehow we can come to accept it. But what happens when people we love, our children in particular, turn out to be mentally ill. I think most of us try to see it as a stage, something they are going through which will soon be over so everyone can get back to normal. Sometimes we are right and everyone relaxes.

Sometimes what we thought was temporary lingers or gets worse. We are faced with accepting that it is not a phase, but the way our child will be for the foreseeable future. I don't know if it matters whether your child is five, sixteen or thirty. Knowledge that they are in the grip of mental illness is devastating. The dreams they had, or which we had for them, seem out the window. Former talents seem to have left them and even a logical conversation may not be possible any more.

What can we do as parents? No matter what happens, it is most important to let our children know we still love them, no matter how bad things get. Sometimes it may seem that they don't even understand what we are saying, but later, when things settle down, they will remember our reminders that we love them.

We can help our children rebuild their lives, and understand how hard it must be for them to do that. I remember casually suggesting to my son that he take a bus to where he needed to be, never realizing that he was terrified of traveling with strangers then, even though he was able to live out of state on his own before being mentally ill.

We can also listen. They may ramble and make little sense to us at times. But being there and showing an interest in them keeps a connection to reality and to society open, even if they are not ready to use it at the time.

What can we do for ourselves? We can remind ourselves that our children's mental illness is not our fault and is not theirs. We had no intention to make our even allow them to be mentally ill. Nor did they choose to become mentally ill or to stay that way.

Feeling grief, similar to losing a loved one through death, is not unusual. We go through the same stages of denial, anger, despair and hopefully resignation and acceptance. Find someone, a relative, friend or counselor to listen to you and help you through the confusion of these feelings and learn to accept yourself and your child as you both are.

What about the future? Sometimes our children pass though mental illness and come out the other side strengthened and fortified, to take on life as they never could before. Sometimes we have to change our expectations and let our children find goals they can reach in light of their current circumstances no matter how limited they may seem to us at the time.

We do not create people and cannot know ahead of time the life purpose of our children. There is already a God in place for that. All we can do is accept our children as doing the best they can and living whatever life they are handed. This is the best we can do for them and for ourselves.

Life Lab Lessons

- Would you think differently about mentally illness if it affected one of your family members?

- What were your dreams for that relative as an infant?

- How would you deal with your embarrassment about the situation?

- What sacrifices would you be willing to make?

- Appreciate the efforts of the mentally ill to cope with their situation.

Joseph G. Langen

No Place to Park

Suicide is a permanent solution to a temporary problem.

~Phil Donahue~

I drove around the funeral home parking lot for some time looking for a spot. I finally parked on the grass. My relatives gathered inside and outside while teens milled around in small groups consoling each other and my cousin's children. My cousin had died by his own hand several days earlier. He left his wife and three children between the ages of fourteen and twenty-two.

What happened? He was a high energy person with many interests and worked feverishly on a variety of projects. On the surface, it was hard to tell there was anything wrong, at least based on casual contact. What could have helped? His sister tried many times to convince him to get help. She knew the toll mental illness had already taken on their family.

Unfortunately, one characteristic of at least some mental illnesses is that you don't know there is anything wrong with you. It can appear that there is something wrong with everyone else.

When we think of mental illness, we often see it as a condition affecting one individual. Even though the brain and mind of only one person is affected, mental illness touches the lives of everyone who cares about that person.

Suicide of a family member is certainly devastating. However, living on a day-to-day basis with your loved one's struggles with mental illness is embarrassing, sad, irritating, depressing, anxiety provoking and conjures up just about every other negative emotion you can think of.

In addition to all the practical problems is the feeling of guilt. Maybe you could have done something to prevent it. You might feel anger at the disruption it has caused in your own life. You might feel sad about losing the company of a once vibrant family member.

All of these feelings are even more difficult to manage alone. If you feel you can't talk with other family members or are ashamed to share the family secret, you have only the company of your own thoughts which are often not very comforting.

Mental health providers are beginning to recognize the effect on families and are also starting to see families as a resource for helping their loved ones cope with mental illness. The Family Institute at the University of Rochester Medical Center is currently developing a program to help mental health providers more effectively involve family members in working with and supporting their loved ones. There are also agencies such as the Mental Health Association which can provide support and information and the National Alliance for Mental Illness providing support services for and by family members. Fortunately, families are starting to be recognized as affected by mental illness and also as resources for their loved ones.

Life Lab Lessons

- If you have a family member with mental illness, ask him or her to tell you about it.

- Talk with other family members to see how you can work together in the interest of your loved one.

- Learn what you can about mental illness.

- With your loved one's permission, talk with his or her therapist to see how you can help.

- Explore family support through associations such as the National Alliance for Mental Illness.

Joseph G. Langen

Chapter 12

Handling Toxic People

While we can tolerate a variety of people, some are more than we can bear. But most of us like to avoid hurting feelings, especially of those who can be vindictive. Tread carefully.

*****

The Idea of Evil

Such is the human race, often it seems a pity
that Noah didn't miss the boat.

~Mark Twain~

Did you ever wonder why there is evil in the world? What is evil, anyway? It is not easy to define. One medieval definition describes evil as the absence of good. Good isn't so easy to define either. We all seem to have a sense of what evil means to us even though it might be hard to put into words. The dictionary defines evil as the fact of suffering, misfortune and wrongdoing, a cosmic evil force or something that brings sorrow, distress or calamity.

Some Muslim leaders have referred to our country as the evil enemy of their religion. Our president has called several countries an Axis of Evil. When you get right down to it, evil means something we detest and see as a threat to our way of life.

How can two different ways of life both be evil? Is one way right and the other wrong? Could it be that people with different views of life think they alone are right and others wrong?

Being different does not make beliefs right or wrong. I remember attending a Catholic elementary school. Across the street was Barnard Elementary School, a public school we referred to as the "Protestant School" although Catholic, Jewish and perhaps other religious views as well as Protestant were represented as well. Looking back, it is easy to see that we saw ourselves as righteous, just and saved while those across the street were ignorant, wrong and doomed.

Children usually think in black and white terms. People are good or bad, nice or nasty, smart or dumb. There is no room for shades of gray. Everything is clear cut.

As we mature, hopefully we find that things are not quite as simple as we thought. People can do bad things but have some good qualities, although it is still easy to think of people in global terms without making distinctions. When I taught college courses at Attica Correctional Facility, I was warned not to tell people I was teaching there because many thought it was a waste of time. They also held that prisoners did not deserve an education. I discovered that among my students, some were in class to avoid boredom. Some were just curious. Some wanted to make changes in their lives. Shades of gray like any college program.

Being different from us does not mean being evil. People with very different religious or political views from our own still have dreams they pursue, families they love and children they cherish, just as we do. They may have the same goals we do although they have a different way of pursuing or expressing them.

From what I can tell, there is no easy way to get beyond our prejudices and see the good in other people who seem very different from us. Perhaps the challenge of living in a diverse world is to find a way to meet our life goals while seeing the good in those different from us and helping them pursue their own goals in their own way.

Life Lab Lessons

- How do you define good and evil?

- How do you decide which category various people, beliefs and actions fall into?

- What do you use as criteria to sort out what you consider good and evil?

- Have you changed any of your ideas about good and evil since you were a child?

- Are you becoming more or less tolerant and you grow older?

Dealing With Ignorance and Stupidity

The highest form of ignorance is when you reject something you don't know anything about.

~Wayne Dyer~

I was asked to write about ignorance and how it makes life difficult. I don't especially like to think about ignorance or stupidity. People tend to use these two terms interchangeably, usually in a negative fashion. However, in my mind, they are not the same thing. I see ignorance as not knowing any better and stupidity as choosing to ignore readily available information.

I once heard a statement, "My mind's made up. Don't confuse me with facts." This approach is used by people who choose not to consider options, alternatives and consequences. There seem to be a number of reasons why people live their lives this way. Or maybe it isn't a choice but just acting mindlessly.

There are people who were brought up to ignore others' needs. They don't seem to realize the effect they have on others and go about their lives, blindly unaware of what it is like for people near them. They can be a pain to live with but stay tucked in their own world in blissful ignorance, usually unaware of how people react to them. Relationships with these individuals are usually rocky. Unfortunately such people can cause chaos at work, in the community and at various levels of government if they get the chance to wield power.

I don't like to think of people as stupid, but unfortunately they are a fact of life. These are the people who should know better, but choose to remain stuck in destructive and annoying ways of living. This category includes bigots, bullies, and selfish people who think only of themselves. My experience has been that they are usually motivated by fear or anger.

People who have been hurt tend to avoid stretching themselves beyond their own comfortable little spaces. They wear blinders and prefer not to know what lies beyond their own experience. They think that what they don't know won't hurt them, so the less they know the better. Such people have been described as leading lives of quiet desperation.

Others have had unpleasant experiences which lead them to feel angry at the rest of the world. Their opinion is that they have been wronged by others and, as a result, they don't owe anyone anything and are owed compensation. They don't usually interact well and tend to take what they want without considering the consequences for anyone but themselves.

Ignorant and stupid people are usually more of a problem for the rest of us than for themselves. There are times when such people may wonder why others avoid them. They may even consider ways to change if they get lonely enough.

It is hard for them to appreciate how they affect the rest of us. Any comments we make are taken as an attack, giving them reason to fear or hate us. Perhaps the best alternative we have is to live in a way which respects others' needs, hopefully setting a good example. The other approach is to keep our distance and not allow their ways to poison our lives.

Life Lab Lessons:

- Are there any areas of your life about which you are being ignorant or stupid?

- How can you learn to make more informed choices?

- What effect does your way of life have on those around you?

- Do you tend to take others' ignorance personally?

- How can you set a good example for people who bother you?

The Gentle Art of Setting Limits

It is impossible to have a healthy relationship with someone who has no boundaries, with someone who cannot communicate directly, and honestly. Learning how to set boundaries is a necessary step in learning to be a friend to ourselves. It is our responsibility to take care of ourselves - to protect ourselves when it is necessary. It is impossible to learn to be loving to ourselves without owning our self- and owning our rights and responsibilities as co-creators of our lives.

~Robert Burney~

Some people bark like dogs when others get too close to their territory. Some people don't know enough to object when others trample on them.

Most of us have our own territory, beliefs or feelings which we cherish and would like others to respect. Would you appreciate strangers walking into your house unannounced? Would you enjoy someone hitting you if they did not agree with you? Do you like being insulted? All these are examples of situations where setting limits is appropriate.

Boundaries are another term for limits and might be a little easier to understand. Football, baseball and soccer all have boundaries. Things that happen outside the boundaries don't count. In setting personal boundaries, you decide what is and is not allowed inside your territory. You don't dictate what someone else does when you are not around. You just decide what is acceptable in your space.

Some people have a hard time asserting their rights. They act as if anything is acceptable and don't stand up for themselves. They expect others to know their needs and wishes and to act appropriately. Unfortunately this does not always happen. Some people don't stop to think what others need or even want. They go about their business doing whatever they please regardless of the effect on others.

We have the choice of letting them walk over us and gritting our teeth, hoping they will some day learn a different way to act. We also have the choice of setting limits. So how do we do it if we are tired of being walked on?

First we need to know what is important to us. Some things people do are annoying but they are not a big deal and not worth making a fuss over. Other actions are very offensive to us or contrary to our most cherished beliefs. We have to decide if it is important enough to make an issue of. Choose your battles.

If it is important enough, we have several options. Attacking them is not likely to be too effective especially if we want to continue having them as friends. We could start by telling them gently about what is important to us and how we feel when our values are not respected. Sometimes a gentle hint is all that is needed. Sometimes it takes a few reminders.

If people don't take the hint, we might need to be clearer about our needs and why they are important to us. If that is not enough, the last resort is to end our association with them. This is a drastic step, but the alternative is giving up our self respect.

Life Lab Lessons

- List some of your most important values.
- Do you stand up for what is important to you?
- If not, why not try a gentle suggestion, or more forceful approach when needed?
- Think about how important your self respect is to you.
- If you don't respect yourself, who else will respect you?

Chapter 13

Navigating Conflicting Values

With the billions of people in the world, diversity of values is not surprising. We will not consider all these conflicts. The possibilities are endless. Here is a sampling of issues which tend to divide us and some ways to think about them.

*****

As God Is My Weapon

He who fights with monsters might take care lest he thereby become a monster. And if you gaze for long into an abyss, the abyss gazes also into you.

~Friedrich Nietzsche~

God has been seen in many ways over the ages. Early people saw the wonders in nature and came to worship the God who was responsible for them. The Israelites came to see God as the Creator who participated actively in their history. The Greeks saw God as the explanation for ideas and the forces of nature. Christians argued about the nature of God for several centuries and finally agreed on God as a Holy Trinity. Christian sects have continued to disagree about their understanding of God, leading to quite a variety of beliefs among churches, all viewing themselves as Christian. Islam originally saw God as requiring its adherents to create a just, equitable society. Eastern religions have had a variety of ways of thinking about God. Karen Armstrong, in *A History of God*, details the development of Jewish, Christian and Muslim conceptions of God.

181

God has been seen variously as Creator, Authority, Protector, Father and Lover. The purpose for having an idea of God is to explain where we and the universe came from and to give us a direction for our lives. God has served as the object of our gratitude in good times and the source of comfort in bad times. Many people who have found their lives drifting have discovered meaning in the context of their relationship with God.

Many of the world's religions, including Judaism, Christianity and Islam have thought from time to time that they had the corner on God. They saw themselves as worshiping the one, true God, while everyone else was in error. They thought God would reward them for their allegiance and punish everyone else for their perversity.

Many religions have taken it upon themselves to convert, subjugate or even kill those who did not believe as they did, all in the name of God. How do people get from a loving God to one who wants us to kill each other?

Although I don't presume to speak for God, it is hard to imagine a divine message for us to destroy each other. My sense is that our faith becomes diluted by our shortcomings and fears. We project onto God our need to feel protected and our need to justify our way of life. We think we are right and "they" are wrong. Our own frailties and insecurities make us think of the God we know as belonging to us alone. Many of the wars fought throughout history have been in the name of God, or at least in the name of differing understandings of God.

Religious adherents and those who seek God on their own need to remember that God does not take sides and does not prefer one religion over another. Many people throughout the world have struggled to make sense of their lives and understand a God who gives meaning to their lives. Our challenge is to find the communalities in our religions and in our search for God. We need to help each other find meaning in our lives in the context of our various understandings of God.

Life Lab Lessons:

- Has anyone tried to use God as a weapon against you?
- Have you ever done it to anyone else?

- If you were God, how would you like people fighting and killing each other in your name?

- Remember that God doesn't belong to any one religion regardless of what its adherents might think.

- Be as respectful of others' beliefs as you want them to be of yours.

Understanding What Gays Want from Marriage

I have great hopes that we shall love each other all our lives as much as if we had never married at all.

~Lord Byron~

Newspapers and magazines have recently been filled with articles pondering the issue of marriage for gays. It has not been at all clear to some what the issues are. Nor is it clear to them what gay people want and why some people object.

Part of the confusion is the meaning of the word marriage. In civil terms, marriage means a legal contract with various rights and responsibilities. Whether a marriage is performed in a church, synagogue, on the beach or at city hall, a marriage contract is signed and has meaning in terms of federal and state laws. Another aspect is the meaning of marriage within particular religions, carrying specific rights and responsibilities within the context of that religion. Although a religious ceremony and civil contract often take place at the same time, they are separate and have different implications. But what do gays want and why do some people object?

In my reading about the issue, it appears that gays are interested in two issues. One is a guarantee of the same rights afforded to heterosexual couples who enter into a civil marriage contract. There are numerous federal laws which relate to being married. Some of them are survivor benefits, immigration and nationality, health insurance, employee and dependent compensation, retirement benefits, Social Security benefits, property ownership, child custody and responsibility, and tax benefits. In addition to equal protection affording them access to legal benefits, gays are also interested in making a public proclamation of their commitment to each other.

What are the objections? Most of these are stated in terms of religious beliefs. Biblical injunctions against homosexuality are often cited. However, state and federal laws are not based on the bible and are specifically drawn up to be independent of religious beliefs.

Homosexuality is also felt by some to be unnatural. However, in the world of nature, same-sex behavior takes place between animals and some species even show long term same-sex bonding. They seem not to have studied the "natural law."

It has also been stated that marriage between gay people will undermine the institution of marriage. No doubt, allowing gays to marry will shake up the institution of marriage. Maybe that is not such a bad thing considering the current state of marriage and its relative instability in our culture.

How can all this be resolved? Since we are talking about civil and religious contracts, it might be best to separate them. We might need new terms for each to avoid the confusion caused by calling both of them marriage.

The civil contract would be available to any two people willing to enter into it, regardless of gender, and convey the current rights and responsibilities of civil marriage. A religious marriage would be understood as separate from the civil contract and would involve the rights and responsibilities bestowed by the particular religion conferring it. If gays wanted a religious ceremony in addition to the civil contract, it would be up to them to find a religion which recognizes their union.

Life Lab Lessons

- What does marriage mean to you?
- Do you realize how marriage has changed over the years?
- Remember that civil and religious definitions of marriage are quite different.

- Could gay people do any worse with marriage than straight people have?

- How have gays undermined your marriage or that of someone you know?

Starting to Understand Wandering Sexual Urges

*Whipping and abuse are like laudanum;
you have to double the dose as the sensibilities decline.*

~Harriet Beecher Stowe~

I was as surprised as anyone about recent revelations of Governor Spitzer's dalliances. I have tried to understand sexual deviation since I worked in a sex abuse treatment program in the 1980's. I was well aware of the public anger, disgust and desire for punishment which followed revelations of such behavior.

More recently, the priest sex abuse scandal resurrected the same reactions which I saw in the 1980's. Indignation arose over clergy who had made celibacy a conscious choice but who betrayed the trust of their church and congregation. It became apparent that it was not just a problem for certain priests but also clergy of other faiths and lay workers as well as volunteers of various faiths.

Lately we have heard about cases of teachers and educators following the same path. Recent news also suggests that almost half of teenagers are sexually active and forty percent of those who are active have sexually transmitted diseases.

Public reaction to all this has generated much more heat than light. People quickly rush to judgment and condemn the transgressors. Seldom do most of us stop to wonder why all this is happening. Easy explanations are rampant. Television is too focused on sexual attraction. It's really not about sex. It's about power. It's a matter of aggression. Teens are not taught abstinence. Teens are taught abstinence.

Over the past few years, I have considered writing a book of interviews of abusive priests in order to understand what motivates their behavior as a way to begin understanding other kinds of sexually inappropriate behavior. For various reasons, I was not able to pursue this project and instead wrote a novel, The Pastor's Inferno, exploring possible explanations based on what I had learned about the subject.

What have I learned? There is no easy explanation. Sexually inappropriate behavior does not have the same motivation for everyone. Predators prey on the weak and take advantage of them without regard for their victims. Some people don't know how to establish an appropriate relationship and seek whomever they can find as a substitute. Some are looking for affection but don't know how to find it, turning to sex as a substitute for closeness. Some people have a very low opinion of themselves and try to feel important by dominating others as often happens with rape.

There may well be other factors which are present in the same individual, further complicating attempts at understanding. Why should we bother trying to understand those who disgust us? As with health problems, mental illness, addictions and many other issues which have plagued us, learning to understand them has helped us know what to do about them. Perhaps the same is true of sexual deviation. Maybe we can all learn to be a little more understanding.

Life Lab Lessons

- Think about things you have done in your life you are not proud of.

- How much control did you have over your behavior?

- If what you did was wrong, how did you decide to do it anyway?

- If it made you feel guilty, did you repeat it?

- If you got it under control, how did you do it?

Priest Sexual Abuse- Why Does It Happen?

*We now have a clearer understanding of what we have
accomplished and what more needs to be done to strengthen
both our child protection programs and our outreach to those
who have been harmed as a result of clergy sexual abuse.*

~Cardinal O'Malley~

When the scandal involving Catholic priests first made the
headlines, my initial question was why. Was there something
about priests which inclined them to be abusive? Was celibacy
the problem? How could men dedicated to service of others
betray their parishioners?

I waited for an explanation. None emerged. Shock, disbelief and
outrage all understandably took center stage. Some people
blamed the Catholic Church. Some tried to minimize the
problem. Bishops covered it up by moving abusive priests like
checkers on a board, hoping they would remain hidden.

Authors and reporters have thoroughly chronicled the effect on
victims. The courts have demanded accountability through
prison sentences for priests and financial penalties for the
dioceses involved. It seemed that this crisis suddenly emerged in
the past few decades. But church documents chronicle attempts
to correct this problem in the first few centuries. It's not a new
problem but a taboo topic as incest was before the 1970's.

So now what? Pope Benedict has pronounced that he will
prevent future abuse by priests without saying exactly how he
and the church hierarchy will go about the task. One of my main
concerns is that in our rush to end the problem we have not first
stopped to understand it. Of course, discussion of sexual abuse is
unpalatable. No one wants to imagine it could even happen. Yet
it does. Although there might be fewer cases lately, priest sexual
abuse still shows up in the news on a regular basis.

Where do we start? The John Jay Commission has taken an
overview of the problem. Now it is time to look more closely at
the contributing factors. What inclines people to abuse others,
particularly children and adolescents? What is there about our
culture which encourages sexual abuse? Is there something about
the structure of the church which encourages priests to become

abusive or attracts potential abusers to the priesthood? What role does the expectation of celibacy play? Research and speculation have explored all of these issues or at least begun the search for them.

The mind of the abusive priest is one resource which has been studiously overlooked. Of course it would be uncomfortable to get into their minds. It would be like wallowing in a cesspool. But maybe that's where some good clues to this problem might appear.

In researching material for my novel, *The Pastor's Inferno*, I was able to find only one study of the minds of molesters, *Unspeakable Acts: Why Men Sexually Abuse Children* by Douglas Pryor. I found no studies of the inner workings of abusive priests. Maybe it is time we as a society open this chapter.

Very little is written about why priests turn to sexual abuse. Actually, there is not much written about why sexual abuse happens at all. Simplified explanations fall short. I refer here to the abuser as male, although there are also some female abusers. However, we are mainly talking about Catholic priests. David Finkelhor wrote a book in the 1980's, *Child Sexual Abuse*, which presented a model with four preconditions for sexual abuse. This applies to all sexual abuse of children, including incest. I was not able to find any better explanation in my travels around the Internet.

The first precondition is motivation to sexually abuse. In order for this condition to be met, the abuser must find himself emotionally compatible with approaching children, which may involve being dominant, more powerful, or comfortable with a younger, smaller victim. He must also be sexually aroused by children. Sexual arousal is different from emotional needs. This sexual arousal often develops during the abuser's childhood sexual experiences with others. The abuser may also find it difficult to meet his emotional and sexual needs in adult relationships.

The second precondition is overcoming internal inhibition. The abuser might be restrained from abuse under normal circumstances. However, he may be less restrained under the influence of alcohol or may suffer from impulse control disorder as a personality trait. Pornography, weak criminal sanctions in society and inability to identify with children's needs may also make a contribution.

The third precondition is overcoming external inhibitions. These include lack of careful parental supervision and unusual opportunities to be alone with children.

The fourth precondition is overcoming the child's resistance. Children who become victims are often emotionally insecure, and/or lacking in knowledge of sexual abuse. There may be an unusual trust between the child and the abuser. The social powerlessness of children can also be a factor.

Only one of these preconditions has to do with being married. Celibate clergy have no access to the normal sexual outlet in marriage, although this is by their own choice. There is nothing in these conditions referring to homosexuality. Studies by Nicholas Groth and others have found that pedophiles are not attracted to adult males or females but rather to children.

Being a priest does not automatically incline one toward sexual abuse of children. The great majority of priests do not engage in such behavior. The statistics on the actual rate of abuse by priests are rather shaky. The rate often quoted is about two percent. It is not clear how this rate compares to clergy in other denominations or to people in general.

Finkelhor's model implies some ways to treat and prevent sexual abuse by priests. One is addressing motivational factors in the course of seminary training, through attention to sexual development and maturity of priests. Another is strengthening internal inhibitions by addressing tendencies to alcoholism, screening for personality disorders and other psychiatric problems, as well as sensitizing them to children's emotional needs. The third is limiting opportunities for priests to be alone with children. The fourth is to help vulnerable children improve self-esteem and learn self protection.

Life Lab Lessons

- Is there something in your past life which shames you?
- What led you to act this way?
- Did you try to stop yourself?

- What kept you from controlling yourself?
- What have you done to get back on the right path?

The Gift of Prosperity

*Prosperity depends more on wanting what you have
than having what you want.*

~Geoffrey F. Abert~

Have you ever thought about what prosperity really means. The government and the news media tell us about lower unemployment, higher wages and the ability to buy more things or spend more money on vacations. It is as if a dollar amount can measure prosperity. But do money and things make us prosperous? Was Howard Hughes prosperous? Maybe on paper. I have come to see prosperity as a state of mind rather than of the wallet or bank account.

I would like to share my journey toward prosperity. My father worried all his life about whether he would have enough money to provide for us, whether he would lose his job or whether he would be poor in retirement. None of these things happened and he always had enough money although he always worried about it. My mother inherited from her parents a healthy respect for money, provided well for us and taught us to respect our money and possessions. We were exposed to two opposing views of money and wealth.

At age thirteen I entered the Catholic seminary and began to learn about the vow of poverty. No one owned possessions in the seminary but we held things in common or had more personal things set aside for our individual use. No one worried about whether mine is better than yours and we all learned a healthy respect for community property.

When I left the seminary at age twenty three, I had to take care of myself for the first time in my life. I had two hundred dollars to my name and no immediate prospects for any more money. I borrowed money for college and living expenses and married without much thought as to where I would find the money to support my family. I bought or charged what I thought I needed, expecting my future income to bail me out.

I managed to increase my debt, sometimes for legitimate reasons, sometimes not. I thought I had to rely on myself. I concentrated on getting more money and not letting what I had get away from me. I clung tight to my money, hoping to survive. The closer I gripped my little bit of wealth, the more it seemed to slip through my fingers.

I started making some changes, but too late. My marriage ended and I found myself bankrupt. I learned from others' experience that bankruptcy could be only a temporary halt to a downward spiral. I knew if I went along the same way I had in the past, I would probably end up in a worse situation. I also learned from others it was best to avoid debt and live on a cash basis. This sounded good, but I still had debts and struggled to survive on a daily basis.

Then two things happened to change my life. I met Carol who knew how to live simply, within her means and without attachment to things. She was also generous with her money. In addition, my brother Bob introduced me to Unity Church were I first heard about a spiritual interpretation of prosperity. This idea baffled my at first. I thought prosperity meant being wealthy and not having to worry about money.

I tried to make logical sense of the concept as I had been trained to do in graduate school. Still, I had no idea how I could pay what I saw as overwhelming maintenance after my divorce. I started writing the word prosperity on all my maintenance checks and thought of them as my contribution to the circulation of the wealth in the universe. I doubled what I thought was a comfortable amount to donate to church and looked for ways my money or possessions could benefit others more than me. I was wary at first, but soon found myself enjoying more what I had and worrying less about where the money I needed would come from.

I found myself back in the spirit of my former vow of poverty where things and money are part of God's universe and come my way for my temporary use and enjoyment. I found I could enjoy things much more when I was not clinging to them.

I had come to see prosperity not as related to the state of my bank account, car, house or what I could afford to do. For me, prosperity is living in balance with the riches of God's universe, giving what I can to help others live their lives and enjoying in a non-possessive way the riches coming my way.

I still think it is necessary to work hard, make plans and be organized. But worrying about the future does not help. There are constructive things we can do about the future, but worrying about it is not one of them. With an open mind, I will see what is necessary to do and what is in my best interest.

Hopefully the story of my journey will be of some help to you in considering your own course.

Life Lab Lessons

- Approach the abundance of the world with reverence. It is here to enjoy but not to worship or cling to.

- Prosperity requires priming the pump. No water comes up from a well unless some is first sent down the well to get it started.

- We need a balance of trust and responsibility for the future. While it is useless to fret about the future, it is our job to make reasonable plans.

- Random acts of kindness are contagious. If we are there in someone's time of financial need or even when a kindness might brighten another's day, it is more likely someone will be there in our time of need.

- Circulate your treasures. I have had things in my life I really enjoyed. After a while they moved from the center of my life. I can store them hoping my interest will return. I can also find someone who may get as excited as I was about my former treasure, who in receiving it brings me the joy of sharing in their pleasure.

Trying to Live Without Credit

A person who can't pay gets another person who can't pay
to guarantee that he can pay.

~Charles Dickens~

I know I'm not the only one thinking about our economy these days. Like everyone else, I wonder how we got in this mess. I have been of the mind for some time that there is a parallel between how the government runs the country and how most of us live our personal lives.

Al Velshi, a senior business correspondent for CNN described three assumptions which underlie our actions. These are that homes will increase in value over time, wages will rise as time goes by and the value of investments in the stock market will go up over time. If we have jobs, houses and investments and these assumptions are all true, we are tempted to imagine we will have more money in the future than we do now. If that's true, why not borrow money and pay it back later when we have plenty? But what if the assumptions don't turn out to be true for us?

The government also borrows money with the hope of paying it back in the future, most likely when it is someone else's problem. If there isn't enough money, they have the option of printing more or borrowing more.

The approaches of most individuals as well as of the government are firmly rooted in wishful thinking. There was a time when people and governments earned money first and then spent it. Some people and governments have made such an approach a priority.

What if we as individuals and as a nation decide to live on a cash basis without borrowing money for whatever we want? Some people say our economy and society would crumble under such a radical approach. It might not crumble but it would be radically different from our current precarious approach to life.

None of us can create an alternative society by ourselves, but we can live our lives in a different way. Have you ever thought what it would be like to live on a cash basis? That would mean you would buy only what you have the money to pay for. Not money you hope to have, but money you have in hand.

At first blush, this sounds dismal. We have become used to feeling entitled to whatever we want. Why should we do without? Anxiety and stress seem to burden everyone more now than when I started working as a psychologist in the 1970's. I wonder how much of this feeling comes from worry about how we can hang on to all the things we accumulate, especially if we have not paid for them yet.

Would you be any worse off? What would your life be like if you had in hand all the money you have paid in interest throughout your years?

Life Lab Lessons

- Think about what you really need in your life.

- How many of your possessions are luxuries?

- Add up the interest you have paid in the past five years.

- What would you do if you had that money now?

- How would you feel not owning anyone anything?

About the Author

Dr. Langen graduated from the University of Illinois in 1971 with a Ph.D. in Counseling Psychology.

He worked at Temple University Counseling Center offering individual and group therapy for Temple students.

He next worked at De La Salle in Towne, an alternative high school and treatment program for delinquent boys in Philadelphia.

He then moved to Western New York where he worked as Supervising Psychologist at Genesee County Mental Health Services in Batavia, specializing in treatment of teens and alcoholics.

At DePaul Mental Health in Rochester he held the position of Chief Psychologist and Child and Adolescent Team Leader, offering individual, family and group counseling. He also participated in the Child Abuse Treatment Program.

He then entered private practice, offering individual and family therapy with children, teens and adults which he conducted in Williamsville NY and Batavia NY.

He began writing a newsletter for his private practice on commonsense wisdom topics. In 2000, he switched to a biweekly newspaper column at the Daily News in Batavia which he continues to publish. His columns are also published online as **Sliding Otter Newsletter**, available by free subscription at **www.eepurl.com/mSt-P**.

He has published four books. They are all available in eBook format from Amazon Kindle Books. Here is the list:

Commonsense Wisdom for Everyday Life, a collection of reflections on life first published in The Daily News in Batavia.

Young Man of the Cloth, a memoir of his nine years in the Catholic seminary and monastery.

The *Pastor's Inferno*, a novel about an abusive priest coming to terms with his abuse.

Navigating Life: Commonsense Reflections for the Voyage, a second collection of reflections.

Release Your Stress and Reclaim Your Life, a self help book for the body, mind, emotions and soul. It tells you the nature of stress, how it finds you, how it affects you and what you can do about it. Also available in paperback from Amazon.

He also maintains a blog, Chats with My Muse, a dialog with his muse, Calliope about the writing process, its challenges and delights available at **www.slidingotter.wordpress.com**.

Personal Note- I wrote this book to share with you what I have learned about stress through my own personal experience and from my years of working with individuals, families and couples. I think the topics we covered can lead to a more organized and personally fulfilling life for you. If you agree and found this book helpful, please consider writing a review on Amazon. You can do so at the Amazon sales page for this book.

Suggested Readings

Ackerman, Diane. *A Natural History of the Senses*. Vintage, 1991.

Armstrong, Karen. *The Battle for God*. Ballantine, 2001.

Armstrong, Karen. *A History of God*. Ballantine, 1994.

Beattie, Melody. *Codependent No More*. Hazelden, 1990.

Beattie, Melody. *The Language of Letting Go*. Hazelden, 1990.

Berry, Thomas. *Dream of the Earth*. Sierra Club, 2006.

Berry, Thomas. *The Great Work*. Three Rivers Press, 2000.

Bradshaw, John. *Healing the Shame that Binds You*, HCI, 2005.

Fillmore, Charles. *The Twelve Powers of Man*. Unity School of Christianity, 1995.

Finkelhor, David. *Child Sexual Abuse*. Free Press, 1984.

Fisher, Bruce and Atkins, Robert. *Rebuilding When Your Relationship Ends*. Impact 2005.

Freud, Sigmund. *Civilization and Its Discontents*. Norton, 2005.

Irving, John. *A Prayer for Owen Meany*. Modern Library, 2002.

Krakauer, Jon. *Under the Banner of Heaven*. Anchor, 2004.

Langen, Joseph. *Commonsense Wisdom for Everyday Life*. Sliding Otter Publications, 2004.

Langen, Joseph. *The Pastor's Inferno*. Sliding Otter Publications, 2008.

Langen, Joseph. *Young Man of the Cloth*. Sliding Otter Publications, 2005.

Michener, James. *The Source*. Random House, 2002.

Moore, Thomas. *The Re-Enchantment of Everyday Life*. Harper, 1997.

Nouwen, Henri. *The Genesee Diary*. Image 1981.

Paine, Thomas. *Common Sense.* Big Fish, 2006.

Pryor, Douglas. *Unspeakable Acts: Why Men Sexually Abuse Children.* NYU Press, 1999

Salovey, Peter and Brackett, Marc. *Emotional Intelligence: Key Readings on the Mayer and Salovey Model.* Dude, 2004.

Sanders, Mark and Silters, Tia. *I Hope You Dance.* Nelson, 2000.

Teilhard de Chardin, Pierre. *The Phenomenon of Man.* Harper, 1975.

Thoreau, Henry David. *Walden.* Digiroads.com, 2005.

Tolle, Eckhart. *The New Earth.* Penguin, 2008.

Tolle , Eckhart. *The Power of Now.* New World Library, 2004.

Made in the USA
Charleston, SC
14 December 2014